# HERMANN OBERTH:
*Father of Space Travel*

# HERMANN

*Introduction by Hermann Oberth*
*Illustrated with photographs and drawings*

TO  ALLISON   who always finds
some way to solve her problems

# Acknowledgments

THE AUTHOR wishes to thank those who so patiently gave of their time and knowledge in the preparation of this work. She also wishes to thank those who provided illustrations and gave permission to reproduce them. The author is particularly indebted to Dr. Walter Bauer, Dr. John Foisel, Mr. Gordon Forbes, Mrs. Kurt Friede, the German Consulate, Mrs. Frederick Holding, Mr. Willy Ley, the Los Angeles Public Library, Mrs. Katherine McColgan of the Aeronautical Library of the California Institute of Technology, Mr. and Mrs. Frank Mueller, Miss Erika Oberth, Mrs. Martha Rowley, Mr. Don Schneider, Mr. and Mrs. Michael Schuller, Judge B. J. Walters, Dr. Volker Wiedemann, and Dr. Fritz Zwicky.

Quotations from *Man into Space* by Hermann Oberth are used by permission of the publisher, Harper & Row. All others are imaginary but based on fact, except those that are documented in footnotes.

# Contents

# List of Illustrations

**Plate 1.** Hermann Oberth (far right) with his father and younger brother Adolf. (Hermann Oberth)

**Plate 2.** Oberth and his fiancée, Mathilde Hummel. (Hermann Oberth)

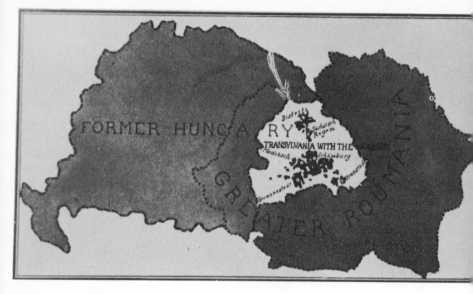

**Plate 3.** The relation of Transylvania to Hungary and Rumania. (John Foisel)

**Plate 4.** The crest of Transylvania, or Siebenbürgen, Dr. Oberth's native province. (John Foisel)

**Plate 5.** Mediasch Central Square, near the school where Oberth taught. (O. Netoliczka)

Plate 7. Drawing of a giant rocket Oberth proposed in 1931. (John Foisel)

Plate 6. Oberth (left), Rudolf Nebel and Klaus Riedel with the liquid-fuel rocket built for the UfA. (Rudolf Nebel)

VIENNA.

ince Jules Verne
te of an imaginary
age to the moon
rtists have dream-
of it as a reality.
ately their dreams
e been taking the
ape of practical
is and experiments
s is largely because
het modern marvel
speed and distance,
rocket

s yet the rocket is
its experimental
ge. But its poten-
lities have been
onstrated to
nt that science
ders the rocket
as the popular
ge of travel in the
far distant future,
sed it not the tre-
ndous advance in
cket experiments
ped Professor Her-
ally to predict that
sible to travel from
half an hour
tific reason
rkable state-
ter in this
neces-
ury of

**Plate 8.** Rocket testing ground at Peenemünde. (A) V-2, (B) mobile test stands, (C) assembly shop. (U.S. Air Force Photo)

**Plate 9.** Oberth and Dr. Dornberger at Peenemünde. (Dr. Walter Dornberger)

**Plate 10.** The first successful V-2 launching at Peenemünde. (Photo released by U.S. Air Force)

**Plate 11.** Peenemünde after the RAF bombing. (Wide World Photo)

**Plate 12.** Underground V-2 assembly line near Nordhausen. (Wide World Photo)

**Plate 13.** Army Ballistics Missile Agency facilities at Huntsville, Alabama. (Wide World Photo)

**Plate 15.** Award to Oberth, showing a cross-section of the *Kegel-duese*. (American Astronautical Society)

**Plate 14.** Oberth at work in Huntsville. (NASA-Marshall Photo)

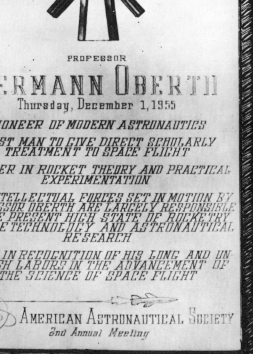

# SPACE FLIGHT AWARD

PROFESSOR

# HERMANN OBERTH

### Thursday, December 1, 1955

*PIONEER OF MODERN ASTRONAUTICS*

*FIRST MAN TO GIVE DIRECT SCHOLARLY
TREATMENT TO SPACE FLIGHT*

*PIONEER IN ROCKET THEORY AND PRACTICAL
EXPERIMENTATION*

*THE INTELLECTUAL FORCES SET IN MOTION BY
PROFESSOR OBERTH ARE LARGELY RESPONSIBLE
FOR THE PRESENT HIGH STATE OF ROCKETRY
MISSILE TECHNOLOGY AND ASTRONAUTICAL
RESEARCH*

*GIVEN IN RECOGNITION OF HIS LONG AND UN-
SELFISH LABORS IN THE ADVANCEMENT OF
THE SCIENCE OF SPACE FLIGHT*

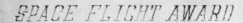

## AMERICAN ASTRONAUTICAL SOCIETY
*2nd Annual Meeting*

**Plate 16.** Oberth and Dr. von Braun. Von Braun holds the Oberth Award presented to him by the American Rocket Society. Oberth is wearing the Great Cross of Merit. (NASA-Marshall Photo)

# Introduction

I AM very grateful that this book is being published in the United States, not so much because it is a personal honor, but because I hope it will be useful for all humanity. The discoveries, inventions, and developments of today are not the work of one nation or one man, but of all countries and all mankind throughout the ages. By concord and agreement, progress is made and science and technology are advanced; by discord, man's efforts are scattered and the products of his work are destroyed.

It is fortunate that the enemies of yesterday have been reconciled, as far as it is possible, for modern rocketry and space flight provide a common task for all mankind. Many nations and innumerable people have contributed to the Space Age. I myself was able to offer the mathematical theory of rocket performance, the theoretical proof of the feasibility of space flight and a discussion of the problem of weightlessness, as well as suggesting and developing such devices as liquid oxygen–alcohol rockets, multistage rockets, regenerative cooling, veil cooling, automatic steering by inertial devices, gyroscopes and servomotors, and the space mirror.* All these were outlined in my first book, *Die Rakete zu den Planetenräumen* ("By Rocket to Interplanetary Space"), first published in 1923.

Other men in other nations have contributed their share to the task of making the theory of space flight a reality. Such things as manned satellites and liquid oxygen–hydrogen rockets, invented and developed by scientists of different countries, today help to show that mankind is becoming a great family, in which each member depends on the others.

There is much to be learned from the world events that occurred during my lifetime. One of the reasons why Germany lost World War II was that too many people, both civilians and military personnel, were interested only in their own advancement. They forgot that no one benefits when personal ambition is realized at the expense of one's country, and that it is sometimes necessary to deny oneself a profit or an honor when it may be harmful to all.

At that time there were also too many learned men who did not understand the importance of long-range rockets and atomic bombs. It is necessary for a modern scientist to study so much in his own specialized field that like the goose stuffed with food, who cries, "God save me from more!" he is often hostile to the new ideas of those in other branches of science.

This state of mind hinders the work of discoverers and inventors and cannot be changed by greater specialization, which, though it may make one's own work easier, also restricts the mind. It is my feeling that better understanding would be possible if scientific material were concentrated into good manuals and further publication were limited by the practice of writing a scientific report only when it offers original material or improves existing material.

* These terms are discussed in the text and can be found in the Glossary—EDITOR

There is something else I would like the reader to notice while reading this biography. I am sure I could have lived more comfortably, especially during my youth, had I worked in the conventional way—had I become a doctor as my parents wished, worked only for financial gain, and done what people wanted of me. However, I would not have been happy! I believe that if one feels called to a certain profession, he should try to follow it without allowing such superficial considerations as position, money, and honors to affect his decision. A man should do the work he enjoys; however, once he has chosen his vocation he should learn it thoroughly and also should not shrink away from difficulty and danger. Henry Ford, in his biography, said that no one should attempt to invent an engine he could not build with his own hands. In 1930 I was given the chance to build a rocket in Berlin, but I was unable to deal with all the practical problems of construction and the rocket was unsuccessful. Afterward, I learned the trades of the locksmith and mechanic. Had I known them earlier, my work in Berlin might have been a success.

Finally, although I do not believe, as men once did, that our earth is a disk surrounded by a bell-shaped sky, over which God and his angels watch to see if we are good, I have come to believe that life is not explainable in terms of matter alone. Man is not merely a machine; he possesses an immortal soul that is the source of the phenomena of life: experience, will, love, and art. The belief that each man must do what he is able has helped to carry me through many difficult times: I have always felt responsible to the Lord for the use I made of the abilities He gave me.

Hermann Oberth
Feucht, West Germany

**CHAPTER 1** ♜ "It is the property of true genius to disturb all settled ideas."

JOHANN WOLFGANG VON GOETHE

# A Christening and a Prophecy [1894]

SUNDAY morning dawned unusually bleak for the latter part of August, 1894. There was a special bustling in certain stone houses along the crooked streets of Hermannstadt, a town in the southeastern part of what was then Hungary and is now Rumania. An important event was about to take place, something which had never happened before and could never happen again. The first-born of Herr Dr. Julius Oberth was to be baptized.

Long before church time the doors of two houses opened and closed quietly in reverence to the Sabbath. Two couples began clomping over streets paved with lumps of stone called "cats' heads." The tilt of their chins would have told a stranger that they came from ancestors not afraid to fight for their land.

"Did you bring our gift?" one wife asked her husband.

He felt for his money bag. It was customary for those attending a christening to take a present for the child, some-

1

thing toward his future career. If a guest could not bring coins he might give a hen to start a flock of chickens to lay the "nest egg" for advanced schooling. Because the burghers or citizens were themselves educated, they planned for their children's schooling.

Dew dripped from the red-tile roofs of gabled houses flanking the streets. When they came to puddles of water, the women lifted their long, full skirts to protect the embroidery and the men pulled back their long white coats made of embroidered sheepskins. All were careful to avoid getting drops on their black hats. These outfits worn on the Sabbath cost many florins and were often inherited.

"I hope we're not late," puffed one of the godparents to his wife. He twisted to see the big clock on the town hall. No doubt the other godparents were on their way. Most christenings had only one or two godparents. Important families had more. It was to be hoped the son of the famous Herr Dr. Oberth deserved four.

One couple moved past a watchtower on the ancient city wall. Those red brick turrets had seen centuries of battle. Migrating from Germany, the Saxons who found this valley put their energy immediately to work molding bricks and mounting stones into buildings. The land soon became known as Siebenbürgen, the Country of Seven Castles. With each castle a church and a wall were built to hold back the barbarous Turks and Tartars. Later the land was called Transylvania, the Land Beyond the Forest.

As they walked the godparents could hear in the distance the tinkle of bells worn by sheep and cattle in the town's pastures outside the wall. Occasionally this music was punctured by the bark of a dog. The sound sent shivers down their spines because all knew that the dogs kept by shepherds were savage brutes. At times in the past they had broken loose and raced into town, their fangs aimed for meat of any kind, be it in cloth or feathers.

Passing the mottled stone house of Herr Dr. Oberth, one wife shifted her gaze to the windows, wondering what was going on behind those lace curtains. A nurse would probably be dressing the month-old baby in his christening robes It was unfortunate that Frau Oberth could not see her first son baptized, but that would not be proper. No woman appeared outside her house after the birth of a child until she had gone through a special purification ceremony at the church, according to Biblical teaching. But the mother could join in the feast after the christening service. Everyone would bring food to her house, fine dishes like wild boar with cranberries and apple fool, a fluffy dessert.

Nearing the church, the godparents moved faster. Though there was no actual work for them to do in advance, they would have to decide where to stand and take their vows of responsibility for the baby. This responsibility would probably not be assumed, as the parents were healthy and there was no sign of another war. After all, most of Europe's rulers were related: Queen Victoria sat on the throne of England, one of her daughters was Empress of Germany and a granddaughter was betrothed to the heir apparent to the Czar's crown. Such family ties guaranteed peace. This new child would learn about war only from history books.

The doors of the church stood open as a sign of welcome. The church had been built after the fashion popular in the fourteenth century by an architect who had one eye on worship and the other on safety. As a result the building was both fortress and church. Probably it was this type of church which had inspired Martin Luther to write his hymn, "A Mighty Fortress is our God." Around the structure was a space where the burghers gathered in case of attack. Circling this space was a high brick wall. Another space and then another wall with watchtowers enclosed the churchyard. So many red bricks had been used that plundering Turks several centuries before had dubbed Hermannstadt the "Red Town."

In the dim cold interior of the church the dark wooden benches against whitewashed walls and the decorated ceiling blackened by centuries added to the effect of strength and timelessness. In a wing built in the fifteenth century the ghosts of Saxon warriors might lurk awaiting the baptism.

Gradually the godparents gathered in a circle. They accepted seriously the responsibility which could fall upon them if tragedy struck the infant's home. Their faces were somber in the rainbow light of stained-glass windows.

"I will see that the little boy attends the *Gymnasium*," volunteered the town burgomaster, or mayor. "The humanistic *Gymnasium*," he added, and the others nodded in agreement that he had chosen the best.

In Transylvania *Gymnasiums* were not to train the muscles but the mind. They were more like private schools and were rated superior to the free community classes. Though most *Gymnasiums* did not snub such subjects as mathematics and physics, they put more stress on cultural learning: languages, religion, and philosophy. A *Gymnasium* which focused on natural and technical sciences was known as a *Real-gymnasium*, but such institutions were rare. Little emphasis was placed on science in schools at that time.

After a short pause the burgomaster's wife spoke.

"I will see that the child is properly clothed."

The others nodded in witness to the sacred vow. The second godfather started to speak, but abruptly halted to stare at the doorway. He blinked as though to clear his vision. This could not be real. Yet it was. A gypsy! On his back hung a large kettle which marked him as belonging to the wandering band that mended pots for Dr. Oberth's hospital. To honor the occasion the fellow had put on a tall hat, a "cylinder" made of astrakhan fur.

"What do you want?" demanded the burgomaster.

"I bring gift." As the man shuffled forward his clothing wafted the odor of onions, grease, and stale sweat. He held out a wooden spoon of the sort his tribe carved to sell when town pockets were buttoned too tightly against "borrowing" hands.

The godparents stepped backward. Undaunted, the gypsy advanced.

"Spoon means plenty. Plenty travel. Plenty fame." He forced the gift into the burgomaster's hand, turned, and left the church.

Stunned, the group stared at the gift grimy with the bear grease that gypsies used to ease all ills, whether of body or of wagon wheel. From high in the church tower the bells began to call members to service. The sound reminded the godparents of the need for haste.

"As I was about to say," continued the man interrupted by the gypsy, "I will help the child become a famous doctor like his father."

Before anyone could reply, a guffaw sounded from the doorway. A giant man filled the entrance. In his shaggy sheepskin coat he resembled a prehistoric monster. One hairy arm held a tight rein on a dog that strained savagely at its leash, fangs poised for attack.

The women scurried to safety behind the benches. The intruder was no stranger, but none had expected to meet him in church. Herr Karter lived outside the pale of religion, though if he knew he was an outcast he paid no attention to the fact. He was the village mystery. When not herding his black *puszta* cattle, he often wandered into town, his quick smile in his brown beard as startling as a white picket fence suddenly appearing in a burned hedge. His flow of words betrayed an education, yet when quizzed about his background his reply was always the same.

"Just a shepherd I am."

Although for years the citizens had been suspicious of him, the children assumed another attitude. Whenever Herr Karter strode into a street he soon had an audience of boyish faces begging for stories of his adventures on mountain peaks. Their favorite tale concerned strange lights high over Switzerland.

"*Ja!*" he insisted. "With my own eyes I saw them hover like sky wagons. They darted up, down, up, and away faster than wind."

When the children startled their parents with this yarn of wagons in the sky the parents called it a new Grimms' fairy tale. They had no way of knowing that half a century later the son of their Dr. Oberth would write about such lights, calling them flying saucers from other worlds.

But now the inventor of this weird story stood in the town's most sacred doorway. The godparents waited, indignant, not daring to move lest the dog break his leash. Herr Karter was the first to speak, his voice booming above the bells.

"So you'll turn the baby into a doctor, eh?" He cocked his bushy chin. "Suppose he doesn't want to juggle a pill and a scalpel? Has he nothing to say about his own life?"

"For your information, Herr Karter," spoke the burgomaster, "the first son does not *have* to follow his father, but he usually does."

"What bad luck to be the first-born! Well, I brought something to change his luck." From under his mangy coat he drew a string of garlic tied into a loop. "Here!" He passed it to the nearest godfather. "May the little son of Hermannstadt find his place in the world, whether on the ground or in the sky." He bowed with elegance and disappeared as abruptly as he had arrived. Only the bells broke the silence in the sacred building.

"Ground or sky!" whispered one godmother. "Did he mean that the baby might die?"

"No! No!" assured the burgomaster. "The fellow's been reading some Jules Verne nonsense." Other citizens were arriving for the morning worship, and he lowered his voice. "Let us take our places."

Since it was customary for women to sit together, the godmothers moved to their side of the church. One touched the arm of the burgomaster's wife.

"You stand next to the baby," came the whispered order. "And don't forget! You know what!"

The wife of the burgomaster knew the ancient superstition that an infant who did not cry at his christening was too angelic to live. Yet did she dare pinch the baby of famous Herr Dr. Oberth? As she was trying to assemble enough courage she heard a second whisper.

"Pinch him to become a doctor. No sky nonsense!"

**CHAPTER 2**  ♜  "Genius is that which possesses a man; talent is that which he possesses."

UNKNOWN

# Dreams of Flying to the Moon [1895-1905]

B Y THE TIME little Hermann had celebrated two birthdays, the women of Hermannstadt gossiped with alarm. Mischief was that child's right name. The curiosity behind his brown eyes would lead to no good. Indeed, every family should help keep an eye on him, or he might even try to fly.

Just as the neighbors were accepting this responsibility, the boy's father made a public announcement. He had been invited to become director of the hospital at Schaessburg, another town in Transylvania, several miles northeast of Hermannstadt. It was a fine promotion, and much as the men dreaded to lose their local doctor they appreciated this honor. The appointment as head of a county hospital was recognition of Dr. Oberth's ability. The women of the town had other ideas. Schaessburg was no place to bring up an adventurous boy: the treacherous Grosse Kockel River flowed by the town. Its bitter yellow water looked harmless near the grassy banks, but it hid deadly whirlpools. Even good swimmers had been drowned.

"Keep that child on a leash!" warned close friends as the Oberths said good-by. "He has too much curiosity."

Frau Oberth received the advice with her quiet smile. She had already investigated her new home, which was near her husband's hospital and had such modern luxuries as a sewerage system. Also, the town had a public swimming pool where children were taught by a lifeguard. As for her son's curiosity, she intended to divert it to the books in her girlhood library. With these she could lead young Hermann into the mysteries of nature: flowers, animals, and the amazing human body. Such knowledge would surely lead to an interest in anatomy and then to the healing art. Eventually, he would join his father's staff. That the boy might have different ideas was unthinkable. Plans for his medical career had been spooned into him with his first solid food.

About the time the boy was learning to identify wildflowers on walks with his mother, he was plunged into consternation by the arrival of a baby brother. His mother became too busy to play with him. Gradually the young boy had to make his first decision, whether to stay with familiar things or venture into the unknown. The latter meant going alone. His deep nature made the choice: he would investigate new paths. Little did he dream that this trait would lead him to both fame and heartache.

His sturdy legs carried him to the river to watch the *puszta* cattle in the mud. Sometimes he saw cows with crumpled horns. Every spring he scuffed down the dusty lane to watch the gypsy wagons arrive in town, accompanied by swarms of naked gypsy children and bony dogs. In autumn he trailed the older children up the 174 steps to the *Gymnasium*, which was located among a cluster of ancient buildings on a height called Old Burg. Here the lonely child stood outside the class door and listened to lessons in Greek, Latin, and the subjects that local parents deemed necessary. Gradually he learned to sing the old national anthem of Transylvania, warm with a feeling of patriotic pride, a loyalty he could not understand with his head but only with his heart.

> "Transylvania, our sweet country,
>    Our dear fatherland,
> Be thou saluted in thy beauty;
>    And about all thy sons
> May the bond of unity be twined."

One especially hot spring, after Hermann was six, a strange odor drifted from town to the houses around the hospital, where it was noticed by Dr. Oberth. This did not come from the white acacias lining the fields and streets. With his usual thoroughness he tracked down the source. Cesspools were being emptied into streams to wash up on the banks and kitchen water pipes poured dirty water into the town gutters. At once the doctor moved his family to a cottage on the mountainside at the edge of a forest.

Here Hermann had his share of chores. He carried buckets of feed to the rabbits and chickens the Oberths raised for food. When a hired man chopped wood, the boy gathered the pieces. On special days Mother Oberth took her two sons to town in their carriage to bring back not only food, but also drinking water, since the house had no plumbing.

Despite these chores, Hermann grew restless. He had little interest in farm living. Only the tools in the barn and shed fascinated him, but when he begged to use them he

heard the same answer: "Too sharp for small hands."
Finally, one day he received a new reply.

"Son," said his mother with strange solemnity. "Tools
are not toys. They're for work, not play. Are you sure you
want to begin to work?"

Deep within the boy something awakened, some vague
ambition which was to grow and stay with him forever. He
set his young shoulders, and, too excited to speak, could
only nod his head.

"Very well, son. You've made your choice. Now make
something. It must be useful. And remember! What you
start you must finish."

Hermann bounded for the tool shed. What could he
make? His father provided every comfort: except one. The
family needed something to catch the flies, some with
stingers, that buzzed around their house. So with hammer
and nails he built a fly trap. To his surprise it worked, with
only one disadvantage. Each time an insect was caught, the
trap had to be baited again. But that did not matter, he
had tasted the thrill of inventing, of doing something never
done before, and he had earned praise. Ambition called
him to do something bigger, but when he cast about for
another project, nothing seemed important. Gradually, the
old restlessness returned.

Hoping to help her son occupy a few hours, Mother
Oberth gave him a fieldglass. To her dismay he spent not
hours but days sitting on the porch looking down at the
town. Though she did not realize it, a new world had
opened for Hermann. He focused on trains chugging across
the Kockel Valley. He studied locomotives on their turn-
tables. He watched cars being loaded with boxes from
weaving mills. He saw the engineer signal. A whistle blew.
Like a trained animal the railroad cars glided along a shiny

track toward the pass in the mountains. Where was the train going? he asked himself. He listened to the puffing and tried to guess the kind of engine from the sound. To his amazement he discovered that the sounds changed with the weather. Here was a mystery. Deep within him, the love of research was stirring.

Between trains Hermann pillowed his curly head on the grass and pointed his fieldglass at the sky. More questions came to him. What was beyond all that blue? Other worlds? It seemed odd that nothing fell from the sky except rain-drops and snowflakes. Had he been able to look into his future, he would have seen fire and death falling around him. In late summer he turned his glass on the storks trailing across the sky. One twilight he saw a pair that seemed to be heading for the moon. Again he was excited: if a bird could fly there, surely a man could too. As he was trying to guess the distance he heard his mother's voice.

"Son! Stop wasting hours! If you spend them well you can go as far as you like."

The idea brought Hermann up from the grass. Go as far as he liked! That meant the moon. Of course he would have to build some wings, but first he must draw them. For this he needed a notebook, a secret notebook. Enthusiasm sent him bounding up the porch steps and straight to his mother's desk. Borrowing some paper he folded and sewed it to form small pages. He would carry his notebook with him always. No one must see his drawings of the stork wings until he was ready to build them.

The idea of landing on the moon urged him to new studies. Sneaking from the house after dark he turned his fieldglass on a full moon. He wondered what it was made of, and what the dim markings might be. His father would know. People said the great Dr. Oberth knew everything.

So, when the tall man drove up from the hospital, the boy ran to greet him.

"Papa, what's the moon?"

"A stone ball with mountains."

"Can we go there? Maybe next summer?"

Father Oberth grinned. "Maybe some day somebody will invent a moonship." He patted his son's shoulder. "Maybe you."

Hermann swallowed. "You think I really could?"

"They say a fellow can do anything if he wants to hard enough." Dr. Oberth started wearily toward the house, the boy at his side. "But, son, I fear the moon would be a poor place to practice medicine." He went up the steps.

Hermann lingered outside, staring at the moon. His father believed he could invent a skyship. He continued his planning with mounting self-confidence. Before he built a moonship he must draw it. Would it sail on wings like a stork? Or go up like a balloon? Pulling his notebook from his pocket, he went into the house to sit by a lamp and draw.

Not for an instant did Hermann suspect that all over the world young men were dreaming of space travel. In Germany, a mathematics teacher, Kurt Lasswitz, had started a controversy on this subject with his novel *Auf Zwei Planeten* ("On Two Planets"). In this book he claimed it was possible to escape the pull of the earth's gravity by using a special vehicle. This spaceboat would be driven forward by a series of small backward propulsions. By the time Hermann was eleven, the book was being read in several languages all over Europe. In the United States a youth named Robert H. Goddard was scheming to find a way to reach Mars. While sitting in a cherry tree he had caught a vision of a spaceship large enough to carry a man. When he climbed down, his "life now had a purpose." He meant to turn his dream into something real, to build it in metal.

There was no limit to the height man could fly since the Wright Brothers had gotten humanity off the ground at Kitty Hawk, North Carolina, in 1903. Throughout the world, unknown boys were training for a race into space.

## CHAPTER 3

♜   "Spaceships will eventually be used by everybody."

**WERNHER VON BRAUN**

# *Jules Verne's Spaceship* [1906–1912]

**W**HEN Hermann's mother gave him a book from the library of her childhood, he gasped in astonishment. A girl's book! Then he read the title. How strange for his mother to have this kind of a book. Perhaps she had seen his secret notebook. Surely she did not suspect that he intended to build a moonship. Again he read the title: *From the Earth to the Moon*, by Jules Verne. The boy dropped into a chair to read the work of the great nineteenth-century French writer.

Gradually the sounds around him fell away. He did not hear the clatter of dishes as the hired girl prepared supper. At the table he ate without taste his favorite goulash. Like a sleepwalker he returned to his chair and in a minute was once again with President Barbicane, preparing the *Columbiad* to be shot off into space. He was one of the crew in the nine-foot ball made of foot-thick aluminum. Hermann marveled. Aluminum was so rare that scientists gave little bars of it as gifts. He read on. The missile to be fired from the cannon weighed twenty thousand pounds. It was hard to believe such a weight could be shot to the moon, over two hundred thousand miles away. The gun was to be nine hundred feet long with a barrel six feet thick. Incredible! Since no gun carriage could hold the weight of such a cannon, Barbicane sank it into the earth at a place called Florida.

Hermann did not hear his family leave the room and go to bed. He was in the ball, about to be fired by thousands of pounds of guncotton. The spaceship was stocked with water, food, instruments, and tools, as well as a map of the moon and seeds to plant on arrival. He wondered how he could breathe in airless space. Barbicane had the answer for this too: he had brought abroad white chlorate of potash crystals, which gave off oxygen when heated. To dispose of poisonous dead air, he had provided caustic potash, which absorbed carbon-dioxide gas.

As Hermann was a slow reader, it was days before he finished the book. He had relished every word and read some passages several times. One evening he went outside to study the moon through his fieldglass. He could almost feel himself leaving the earth at the rate of seven miles a second. His scientific mind began to ask questions. Where did Jules Verne get that figure? Was it correct? Would a space traveler really become weightless when the earth's gravity balanced that of the moon? The boy tried to focus on a moon crater. The *Columbiad* might have landed there if its speed had not been retarded by using a rocket as a brake.

That night Hermann could scarcely sleep. The next day he started to read the book again. He read it six times. He drew pictures of the *Columbiad* in his notebook and copied down Verne's calculations. If they were correct, anyone could build a skyship. So could he if he could learn more mathematics. Unfortunately, the *Gymnasium* his parents had selected for him was humanistic, not scientific. Hermann sharpened his pencil. According to what little arithmetic he knew, the calculations of Jules Verne were wrong. Surely an aluminum ball would have been crushed by the gravity of sudden take-off. In desperation Hermann finally went to his teacher.

"Forget the moon!" said Herr Fabini. "You can't go there."

Again the boy faced a decision which was to determine not only his character, but his future. He could either give up trying to do what others said was impossible, going to the moon, or follow his own inner call. It really was no choice. He had to go on with his moon project, even if it meant lonely hours and ridicule.

One idea presented in the Jules Verne story intrigued him. Was it always true, as the seventeenth-century English mathematician Sir Isaac Newton said, that "every action hath an equal and opposite reaction"? To test this theory Hermann went to the river, climbed into a boat, and jumped from it to the grassy bank. At once the boat pushed in the opposite direction. Again and again he tried the experiment, always with the same result, until there was no doubt in his mind. Newton's theory was really a law. Settling under a willow tree, Hermann applied this law to his moon vehicle. If he were to shoot it from a gun, he must know the downward force of the explosion to determine how high the ship would rise. Obviously, he could not use wings. A bullet shape was better than a ball. This idea prompted another question: how could he measure the amount of gunpowder needed? Darkness closed around him as he figured in his notebook.

Supper was over when he reached home, and to make his arrival more embarrassing there was company, the town pharmacist, a special friend of the Oberths. Hermann's mother did not scold him but her face showed that she was vexed. Hermann went sheepishly to the table. It was futile to explain his experiment; she would call it wasted time for a young man destined to become a doctor. He wanted to blurt out his desire to be a scientist, but Saxon boys did not go against their parents' wishes, so there was nothing to do but keep his secret and wait. He knew he would never give up his moonboat. Some day he would build it, of that he felt sure.

When the supper guest was ready to leave, Hermann walked part way with him to carry a lantern. In silence the two moved under a dark sky. Then the pharmacist spoke in a pleading tone.

"Boy, I'll make a deal with you. Quit dreaming in class, get good grades, and I'll let you shoot my triple-barrel gun."

Hermann looked at his friend suspiciously. Such talk sounded like family prompting. Thrilling as it would be to use the gun, he could never give up thinking of his skyship. Still, he would try for better grades, since it meant so much to his family. After an awkward silence they said goodnight. As the boy turned back toward his home the moon rose over the horizon. The triple-barrel gun, the grades, everything was forgotten. Nothing mattered except reaching distant space. He wondered how a skyship would behave when it reached the border between the gravitational pull of the earth and the moon. Perhaps that depended on his fuel. Of course there was nothing better than the gasoline used by horseless carriages, but how would a liquid behave in weightless space? He must experiment.

During the following weeks, a scheme took shape in his mind. Early one Saturday he went to the town's swimming pool, a bowl-like cove in the bank of the river. Because he was an athlete, the lifeguard permitted him to use the high diving board. This time, however, Hermann was not diving for pleasure. In one hand he carried a bottle half filled with water and tightly stoppered. He wanted to learn how the liquid would act at the moment during a dive when he was going neither down nor up, a condition similar to the moment when a skyship was between the pull of the earth's gravity and that of the moon. The success of a space trip might depend on knowing what fuel would do at that moment. Without hesitation he dove.

To his surprise, the water rose around the inner sides of the glass, leaving an air core. Satisfied with this, he asked himself: suppose the skyship needed fuel heavier than water? Going to his friend the pharmacist he borrowed some mercury, or quicksilver. With this tightly corked in a bottle, Hermann dove again. The mercury hung suspended as if it had no weight.

Delighted, he returned the mercury and hurried home. He felt that he was on the way to the moon. However, as weeks flew by a new aspect of space travel confronted him. How, he wondered, would his body function without the usual air pressure on it? Perhaps his heart would go into wild pounding. Perhaps his veins would burst, or his lungs. He must find the answers to these problems.

Months passed, and Hermann grew into a tall, lean young man. Always in the background of his thoughts were his sky problems. One day he decided to experiment again at the pool. Perhaps he could study his body reactions during a dive. For a fraction of a second he would be weightless, as in space, going neither down nor up.

Early in the last day of the summer swimming season, he went to the pool. The air already had the chill of coming winter. The lifeguard wore a warm sweater and shook his head with disapproval when Hermann prepared to go into the cold water.

"Keep your eyes open when you dive!" warned the life-guard. "And don't dive deep!"

"Why not, Herr Henning?"

"Because you must see the light. The cold will chill your nerves. You won't know which way is up."

Hermann did not reply. For a long moment he stood staring at the water, excited thoughts tumbling through his mind. The chill of cold water was nothing compared to the cold of space. In his moonship it might be fatal not to know directions. Perhaps chilling his nerves in the pool would give him an idea of what to expect in space.

He climbed the tower and dove. Nothing happened except that the coldness of the water shocked him. He tried again. On the eleventh dive he became muddled. He could not find the ladder. Never had the pool seemed so murky. With a start he realized that he could not remember which side was up. Terror gripped him. He could not hold his breath much longer.

Nearly unconscious, he felt his hand touch the ladder and managed to pull himself out. Though his muscles quivered from the strain, Hermann trudged home with a degree of satisfaction. He had survived a small taste of the bewilderment of weightlessness. Until he found a way to make a more complete test, he would work on designing his ship. It needed a metal skin and strong fuel tanks. Since there was no information in books on the shape of the tanks, he was forced to experiment.

He borrowed a rubber bag from his father's hospital. Then he borrowed a linen bag from the hired girl and poked the rubber one into it. In the backyard, he filled the rubber with water until it stretched to fit the linen sack. This gave him an idea for an oval fuel tank. Approximately thirty years later he was to work on V-2 rockets at Peene-münde, the center for development and manufacture of

German rockets and robot bombs in World War II. Each rocket had one metal tank of this shape, nicknamed the "Peenemünde Egg."

Every day Hermann searched for ideas to apply to space, always wondering what fuel to use in his ship. Then, in 1911, he found the answer in a book: liquid hydrogen and liquid oxygen. A combination of alcohol and oxygen also had high burning power. Of course, these fuels were dangerous to use. He wondered if passengers could be carried safely in a space craft powered by such fuels. Had he been able to look into the future he would have seen a rocket of his design cross the English Channel driven by alcohol and oxygen. Fifty years later men called astronauts would be able to venture hundreds of miles into space because of the principles he was discovering.

As his last winter in the Schaessburg *Gymnasium* drew toward its close, he was required to write a thesis. To his astonishment the teacher returned it marked, "Not neat. Copy over!" Hermann was disgusted over such wasted time. He argued with the teacher that future writing would all be done on the marvelous machines called typewriters, already in many of the local stores.

"Oberth!" came the stern reply. "Your notions are against tradition and therefore wrong. Copy over!"

Hermann obeyed. But while he was writing he came to a conclusion which was to sustain him through criticism and ridicule. To follow mere tradition was like riding in a car with the headlights behind. He made a resolution: "In the future, before I give up my opinions someone must actually prove them wrong."

At the spring graduation it was customary to have a church service to give thanks for the year's schooling. The boys wore silk berets with ribbons to show their class, and the alumni wore their insignia. It was an affair both gay and reverent. Hermann walked in the procession, only vaguely aware of the ceremony, gazing at the Gothic arch and far beyond. If only he could learn the secrets of the boundless sky. In his classes he had studied philosophy and religion but almost nothing of the subject closest to his future, and perhaps secret, career. He knew that another doctor would be welcomed in the town and that his father looked forward to the day his eldest son would take charge of the hospital. It seemed to mean nothing to his family that he had won a special prize in mathematics. They did not see it as an arrow pointing to engineering or scientific work. Hermann tried to accept his duty. Perhaps in his spare time he could pursue his space dream and some day build his moonship. But now he must become a doctor.

# CHAPTER 4 ♖ "Human history becomes more and more a race between education and catastrophe."

H. G. WELLS

# Sword, Not Scalpel
## [1913-1915]

ERMANN'S shoes felt weighted with lead when in the autumn of 1913 he bid his family good-by. Dr. Julius Oberth made no attempt to conceal his pride that his son, age nineteen, was starting to study medicine in Munich. The elder man, announcing the good news over the town of Schaessburg, did not notice that his son winced whenever the medical career was mentioned. At the depot Hermann's neighbors waved good-by with pride. The young man answered at the coach window, his eyes blinking rapidly, a set smile on his gentle face.

Hermann watched the scenery while the train chugged over the high plateau on which Munich was located. The mountains to the south reminded him of his home town and sharpened his feeling of loneliness. He was now on his own resources; success or failure depended only on him. Never again could he return to his childhood. He must accept a man's responsibility, and begin carving his place in the world, the medical world. If he could save a few hours for his moon vehicle, perhaps he could endure.

When the train stopped, he carried his suitcase down the steps. Munich, with the stir and commotion of industry, was considered a modern city. Draft horses clomped over the cobblestones, pulling carts loaded with pyramids of barrels that gurgled at each sudden halt. Munich beer was advertised as being scientifically brewed, a statement that the people tested on each holiday. Nor did they wait for official holidays. Beer gardens were social centers at night; by day there were "breaks" for beer and sausages.

Hermann walked toward the University, pausing to study the two bronze statues at the entrance: Science and Truth. The truth was, he thought, that he wanted to study only science. With a sigh he moved toward the big door. Through this entry the great German physicist Konrad Röntgen had passed after he had discovered the X ray in 1895. Awe overwhelmed Hermann as he stepped inside. Here was the great hall, or *Aula*, for lectures. And there was the library, which he had heard contained over a half-million books. Among so many volumes there was sure to be one containing the data he needed about distant space. Knowing the exact speed for leaving the earth's atmosphere, for example, was essential. If his rocket flew too rapidly the air resistance would burn it up; if too slowly, its weight would drag it down.

To the young man's delight, the University permitted him to sign for two extra lectures in addition to his medical course. At once he put his name down for mathematics and astronomy.

"But Herr Oberth!" protested Professor Emden, a science teacher. "You're a medical student. I don't understand how you know so much about aerodynamics."

"It's my hobby," explained the boy, trying to sound casual.

Autumn days shortened into winter. Hermann was too busy to become acquainted with many students. Occasionally, for exercise, he walked about the town. He had no reason to guess that one of those beer halls would become famous as the "Brown House" of a political group called the Nazis, nor that on those same streets walked a penniless fellow named Adolf Hitler. Both young men dreamed of a wonderful future. The doctor's son saw travel to the moon. The other saw himself a famous painter.

With the melting of snow, spring hopes began to flower. There was a strange tension in Munich which Hermann felt but could not define. It lay like a shadow over the land. Still, business went on as usual. Everyone had money, especially the tourists from America, whose dollars were each worth four German marks. They bought souvenirs, and talked cheerfully about world conditions, bragging a bit on the side. Yes, Model T automobiles were actually turned out on a new system, the assembly line, at the rate of ninety-three a minute. They smiled at the mention of the Russian revolutionist who called himself simply, N. Lenin; he was a puff of wind against the might of Czar Nicholas II. There was no danger to world peace.

As the school year drew to a close, Hermann received disquieting letters from Schaessburg. Instead of family details he was told that the Balkan states were a "powder keg" which might explode at any minute. He tried to understand the situation. That neighboring Serbia hated Austria-Hungary did not necessarily mean a major war, though there might be a few border skirmishes. Small wars were common in that part of Europe. Boundary lines writhed back and forth like serpents, but life went on the same as always.

By the middle of June 1914, the students at the University were looking forward to summer vacation. Then abruptly all talk focused on an item in the newspaper. Hermann read it a second time, thinking he had made a mistake. It was incredible that an Austrian archduke would announce a visit to Serbia. Especially Archduke Francis Ferdinand! No man was hated by the Serbians more than he.

On June 28, further news broke over a startled world. A "welcoming committee" of Serbians had stationed themselves along the announced route of the Archduke. At the appointed time, the Austrian sedan approached, flags flying. As it turned to cross a bridge, two shots rang out. No more were needed. These two had done more than end a life. They had sent sparks to every arsenal in Europe. A month later Austria-Hungary declared war on Serbia. Neither nation suspected they had lighted a bonfire that would destroy them. Both countries vanished at the end of World War I.

Hermann first heard the news of war while vacationing in Switzerland. Being part of Hungary, Transylvania would have to fight, so with deep loyalty Hermann packed his luggage and started for his homeland. Passing through Austrian towns, he saw flags in the streets and bands on parade playing military marches. Regular troops, marching in formation, sang their national anthem. Hermann's spirits filled with awe and pride. It was hard to believe that bloodshed would come after all this splendor.

Arriving in Schaessburg, he found a different scene. At the depot he was greeted by solemn faces. Old men who had seen previous campaigns spoke in whispers and shook their heads. The parents of young men looked anxiously at their sons, but the eyes of girls shone with admiration for the heroes who had enlisted. Flowers were presented to those setting off for camp.

For days Hermann wandered about the town, trying to fit himself into the picture. The news seemed unreal. France and Russia were standing by little Serbia, and in a short time they found themselves at war with Germany. When Germany invaded Belgium, England entered on the side of France. Bugles were sounding. A race into uniform had begun. In Berlin the Kaiser with his six sons, all in uniform, led a military parade. In Russia, peasants left their plows to join the army in hope of earning a prize of two hundred thousand rubles (one hundred thousand dollars) offered to the first Russian soldier who set his boots in Berlin. In Piccadilly Circus, London boys were marching to the tune of "Tipperary."

Hermann felt a stranger to most of the young men in town, who talked only about the war. To his surprise the girls he had known were now young ladies. He had forgotten that the eyes of one named Mathilde Hummel were the color of the sky. Something in her smile made his blood pulse stronger and gave him a pleasant heady sensation. Then one day he told her that he, too, was going to war. When she nodded approval, he wanted to say that he would make her proud of him, but a sudden shyness held his tongue, and they merely shook hands.

After bidding his family good-by at the depot, Hermann boarded a train for Hermannstadt. He enlisted in the Austro-Hungarian Regiment No. 31 as a foot soldier, not a medical student. He did not thrill when a uniform was assigned to him. With dull emotion he listened to the sergeant's speech.

"The blue-gray of your uniforms blends well with our rocky passes where you'll probably be fighting. Your branch of service shows on the patch of color on your collar. The gold buttons mean you're Hungarians, not Austrians. Come winter, you'll be issued long overcoats. Clear?"

Hermann caught his breath. Winter! Surely the war would not last that long. A shout from the sergeant brought him to attention. With the other boys he started putting on the new uniform. He had difficulty tucking his trousers into the tops of his boots. Soon he was answering another call, this time to train, to learn the trick of handling a gun. Now he understood that this rifle technique was not for display at parades before cheering crowds. No! He was learning to run a bayonet through some fellow like himself. Every inch of his body rebelled, but he was trapped. The only escape was to run away; but how ashamed his father would be of a son who refused to defend Transylvania! Also, Mathilde might think him a coward. He wished he had enlisted in the medical corps, where he could heal wounds instead of inflict them. Now there was nothing to do but wait for peace.

In August Kaiser Wilhelm, Emperor of Germany, had taken the lead in the war against England and her allies, and announced good news. "The war will be over in six weeks."

This news filled Hermann with fresh hope. Soon he would be back at the University, listening to lectures on aerodynamics and in his spare time designing his rocket. The future looked bright.

But the six weeks stretched into months. He finished his training and was sent to the front. Austria-Hungary was beginning to suspect that this was not a lightning war. The Czar had massed his Cossacks—mounted fighters known for their brutality. They were now riding toward the Carpathian Mountains to swarm through its passes. Transylvania was in danger. Every man in Hermann's regiment readied for action.

Reports of other threats to his homeland came soon:

the "pig farmers" of Serbia had become fighting demons, and Rumania, though officially neutral, was casting greedy glances toward the rich lands around Hermannstadt and Schaessburg. Hardly had he recovered from this shock when Hermann received the order to dig in.

Trench warfare was old in the land: the ancient Romans had used it. But until now, to Hermann, "trench" had been merely a word in a book. To his dismay he was ordered to dig a second trench behind the first, then a third. With no regard for aching muscles, instructions were given for connecting channels.

Hermann discovered he was living like a human mole, except that in some ways a mole had the advantage. It could get into a hole to escape the rain: the soldiers could not. Their trenches served as dining room, parlor, and bedroom. Uninvited guests arrived: rats by night, "cooties" or lice at all hours.

Sick at heart and numb from fatigue, Hermann filled every hour from dawn to dark with work. No sooner were the trenches completed than he worked in the area beyond the front trench, a section later called No Man's Land, spreading tangles of barbed wire to slow down a Cossack charge.

As the war dragged on, the citizens of Austria-Hungary began to complain. They had to spend too much time raising food or making munitions for fighting men. To spur patriotism, Hermann's regiment was paraded with full colors and drums (Plate 1). Though excited girls tucked flowers into his gun, the dour faces of adults showed the majority were not in sympathy. Something had to be done to inspire their willingness to make sacrifices.

For the first time the governments on both sides of the war started to publish atrocity tales, as well as the usual catch slogans. The soldiers were taught a song of hate, the "*Hasslied*," to lash their enthusiasm for fighting unseen enemies.

> "French and Russian, they matter not,
> A blow for a blow, a shot for a shot.
> We will never forego our hate,
> We have but a single hate,
> We love as one, we hate as one,
> We have one foe, and one alone,
>                    *England*."

Perhaps the name of England was used because few citizens of Transylvania had ever seen a Britisher. An Englishman could be painted as a demon. Gradually the populace believed this propaganda. Hermann noticed that on parades his regiment was greeted with shouts of "God punish England!" and "Germany above All!"

During this time a plan took shape in his mind. Since England was the principal enemy, the way to stop the war was to cripple London. Suppose one of his rockets were shot across the Channel. That would certainly shock King George into quick terms. No sane country would continue to fight a weapon for which it had no defense. One such rocket might end the World War.

The more Hermann pondered the possibility of stopping the war with his rocket, the more plausible it appeared. Before it could be fired, though, it had to be built; and before it could be built, it had to be drawn to scale. While he was scheming to find time to put his ideas on paper, an accident occurred, and he was wounded. Since he was no longer able to bail out trenches or carry a gun, he was transferred to Number 22 Field Ambulance Unit.

When he bid farewell to his fellow foot-soldiers there was a new light in his dark eyes. In his new job he would find a few minutes to develop his rocket and thus shorten the war. Also, at his new assignment, the military hospital in Schaessburg, he would be near a certain blue-eyed girl. Mathilde would be proud of his rocket, he thought. But suppose she did not approve of it? He wondered if he could give it up for her.

**CHAPTER 5** ♖ "Nothing is impossible in this world. All that is needed is to find a way of carrying out one's plans."

**HERMANN OBERTH**

# Could Rockets End World War I? [1916-1917]

B Y THE SPRING OF 1916 people were fearful that the war would turn into an endurance test. Hermann's regiment settled down to the task of keeping the Czar's Cossacks behind the Carpathian Mountains, which separated Transylvania from Russia. This proved not too difficult, because the seeds of the coming Bolshevik Revolution were already sprouting. Russian peasants rebelled at being whipped by drunken officers, and Russian volunteers demanded real guns instead of sticks, a request their officers were afraid to grant since the bullets might be sent in their direction.

Hermann relished being in the ambulance unit. He found spare time to study mathematics and, unknown to his superior officers, to work on problems of space, particularly the mystery of weightlessness.

Hoping to find a drug that would produce the sensation of weightlessness, he studied pharmacy at the hospital. One alkaloid intrigued him, a poison made from the herb henbane that was used as a sedative. He decided to try it. From his swimming days he knew that the best place to have free movement in all directions was in water. Realizing that there was a danger of his drowning, he asked a friend to stand by.

As he could not go to the river, he filled a tub with water. Then he swallowed a dose of the alkaloid called scopolamine. While waiting for it to take effect he wound a hose around his body, placing one end in his mouth and the other outside the tub in such a way that he could breathe with his face down or up. With unsteady movement he stepped into the water, the drug deadening his nerves. He closed his eyes. Gradually he lost the power to coordinate his actions. He rolled over several times, unable to tell up from down. Panic seized him and for the moment he forgot the experiment. His arms lashed out and his friend helped him from the tub.

Because his scientific mind would not accept a conclusion based only on one trial, Hermann repeated the experiment many times. He had discovered what American pilots were to experience about a quarter of a century later. He wrote it as a fact of space flight: "Weightlessness will first produce a sense of fright. Then a pressure on the throat."

When he later wrote his book, *Wege zur Raumschiffahrt* ("Road to Space Travel"), he included this experiment. "There is an alkaloid, scopolamine, which puts to sleep the organs of balance. This is dangerous. . . . Witches of the Middle Ages produced the same result with a notorious ointment. In both the sense of gravity was deadened."

Not satisfied with this knowledge, Hermann wanted to know if the feeling of weightlessness was harmful. Could it be accepted without panic? It was necessary to know this before man set out into space, so by sly maneuvering he managed to perform more tests. At last he came to a conclusion which he presented in the same book.

"The lowering of gravity on the body for several hours or days could not do any physical harm. All life is possible whether vertical or horizontal."

But Hermann also had military work to do. While on ambulance routine he heard alarming rumors from the soldiers. Rumania was scheming to acquire Transylvania. Rumanian diplomats were shuttling back and forth to Allied headquarters. Though no one knew it, a secret treaty was being signed. In return for entering the war on the side of the Allies, Rumania would receive the prize she wanted, Transylvania. Toward the end of August the news broke into print.

"RUMANIA DECLARES WAR ON AUSTRIA-HUNGARY."

Hermann's hours of rocket study ended abruptly. Rumanian troops were heading for the mountain passes. The Transylvanian soldiers dug additional trenches with shovels, bayonets, cups, or fingers, the enemy scarcely forty miles away.

Soon days and nights became nightmares. The darkness was broken with the flashes of big guns and fireworks of exploding shells, and the air quivered with the sound of machine guns.

Though Hermann's body ached from carrying the wounded, hope sustained him. The war could not last long, as Russia would soon cease to be an enemy. She was collapsing from within, said the Russian peasants who had surrendered. That left only England as a strong opponent, since America would remain neutral and not help King George. The United States had just elected President Wilson on the basis of the slogan, "He kept us out of war." If

Britain could be quelled, the war would stop, and there was a way to accomplish this. A rocket landing on Parliament would force King George to ask for peace. Hermann was determined to find time in which to complete his missile.

By working during the night Hermann drew his rocket to scale. He wrote and rewrote equations for fuel. Though he did not realize it, he was designing the ancestor of the V-2 rocket of World War II. Had Berlin listened, his rocket might have been a victory weapon for Germany in World War I. But the Kaiser had too many other problems to listen to a young sergeant stationed in Transylvania.

Every day Hermann followed the war bulletins. The Kaiser was growing desperate. He had ordered his submarines to "Sink a ship on sight!" Drowning the uninjured was not necessary, thought Hermann. This fighting must cease; he must try harder to perfect his rocket.

To encourage peace, President Wilson offered to negotiate what he called "Peace without victory." Certain of victory, Kaiser Wilhelm refused. His enemy, Russia, was sinking into chaos, her peasant soldiers in wild flight both from German soldiers and from their own blundering officers. With no Cossacks on his eastern front, the Kaiser could throw all his troops against the British "Tommies."

Then a war dispatch arrived that shocked every man in Hermann's unit. The American President had asked the German people to overthrow their Kaiser. Such an idea was treason. The head of their government was a symbol of law, order, and unity.

In March Hermann threw his cap into the air along with others: the war was practically over. The Russian Revolution had forced the Czar from his throne. The Soviet people were in confusion, just as the Kaiser, a shrewd warlord, had expected. To aid the Russian Revolution, he had permitted its leader, Lenin, to cross Germany in a sealed train from

Switzerland, where he had been in exile. Peace, said the Kaiser, would come any day. Hermann was hopeful. His rocket would not be used for war. Soon it could soar off into the peaceful blue, maybe toward the moon.

By April the headlines were no longer hopeful: The United States had declared war on Germany with the excuse that "The world must be made safe for democracy."

After the shock subsided, a sense of despair settled over Hermann and his unit. America was full of young men of military age. To bolster German morale, General Paul von Hindenburg issued a statement sharp with challenge.

"We now have a new enemy. She is the most powerful in the world. But will she prepare and arrive here in time to snatch the victor's laurel from our brow?"

Spies reported that America was not prepared for war. The country had only five camps to train draftees. The supply of military shells was not enough for more than five hours of battle and the country had no machine guns. Many of their rifles were 1903 Springfields. There were only fifty-five planes, unarmed. Officer candidates, it was said, drilled with broomsticks and hurled tomato cans for grenades. Furthermore, American mothers were shouting a song: "I Didn't Raise My Boy to Be a Soldier." Considering all this, Germany had time to win.

Hermann worked on his rocket while his comrades slept, but his secret work was limited. He was summoned with other men for extra drilling. News had come that General Pershing and about two hundred men had sailed for Europe singing "The Yanks Are Coming." American bands played a gay tune, "Over There." All over America young men were putting on khaki and winding their legs with puttees, long strips of cloth that gave their uniforms a trim appearance. British Tommies filled the Channel boats.

In Hermann's world there was no time to sing or parade.

He met the daily problems of wounded, sick, or missing soldiers. In town the civilians worked to provide food for their boys. All shared one hope: to subdue England and end the war before the American Expeditionary Force arrived.

Each minute Hermann could snatch from routine work or from sleep he spent on his rocket. Time after time he changed the formulae for its fuels. It was hard to know whether to have more alcohol or more oxygen. He measured the lines for accuracy and checked the figures. Then one evening he forgot to take his usual precaution against being discovered when he was supposed to be sleeping. A sliver of light from under his door caught the attention of the regimental physician, who came unannounced into the room. Hermann tried to stand in such a way as to hide his papers.

"What's that?" demanded Dr. Otto Csallner, pointing.

"Just a drawing, Herr Regimental Doctor," replied the nervous young officer.

The older man moved to look at the sleek missile with its pointed nose and tail fins. Not being a rocket expert, he understood neither the sketch nor the equations.

"What is this funny thing?" he demanded.

Hermann straightened. "Please, Herr Regimental Doctor, it is top secret."

The officer reared back. "If anything is top secret I know of it. Never heard of this." When the young man remained rigid in silence the doctor softened his voice to an amused tone. "Well, I'll keep your secret. Now explain this drawing of a big skyrocket!"

"Herr Regimental Doctor, it is a rocket for the sky but not like a skyrocket. This is not made of cardboard, nor does it use gunpowder."

The doctor's manner implied both suspicion and doubt. "Well, just exactly what is it?"

Relieved at the chance to unburden his thoughts, Hermann explained. The drawing was something he had invented, a long-range missile that could carry an explosive. It was made of metal and stood about 82 feet high and was approximately 16 feet in diameter.

The doctor collapsed into a chair, his thoughts plainly written on his face. This young man was out of his mind! After a tense moment the older man spoke, a hint of sarcasm in his tone.

"What makes it go? Wind, no doubt."

Although normally Hermann was a slow speaker, now words came rapidly. Air had nothing to do with this rocket. It operated on Newton's law of equal action and reaction. It was driven upward by the rear push of gas downward, the same principle on which a skyrocket operated. But instead of gunpowder burning in a small hole, his rocket had a metal "oven." His fuels, alcohol and oxygen, were injected into the oven where they united to form a gas which shot out as a jet flame. The power of this rear exhaust drove the rocket in the opposite direction. Since it had an automatic steering device, it could be sent anywhere.

"Never heard of such a thing," exclaimed the doctor.

"No, sir, it's something new. I've been inventing it since I was twelve."

Dr. Csallner looked carefully at the young man. Satisfied that the youth was both sober and sincere, he spoke:

"Do you think this thing will really fly?"

"If my calculations are correct, Herr Regimental Doctor, it will travel hundreds of kilometers."

The doctor got up from his chair for another look at the drawing, but its lines and figures still made no sense.

"What's it good for?" he finally asked.

"Sir, one or more sent to England would frighten King George into surrendering and then the war would be over."

The leathered features of the tall officer revealed consternation, doubt, and then a trace of hope.

"If what you say is true we must send your drawing to Berlin. Only Headquarters has the scientists to evaluate it."

"Will it be safe in ordinary mail?" Hermann managed to ask.

Dr. Csallner hesitated. "I'll find a way. In the meantime, show it to nobody!" He abruptly left the room.

That night Hermann lay awake too excited to sleep. If Berlin would give him a laboratory and helpers he could build his rocket. Of course, first he would need to build a model to perfect the technical details. There were many problems he could solve only by testing: He would have to determine the right mixture for his fuels. Suppose the heat of the gas they generated melted his oven? Against the pressure of this gas could he get the fuels into the oven? Certainly they would not flow in by gravity. He would have to use pumps. But, with enough helpers, all these details could be overcome, and then his sleek giant would roar off for London. Later, in time of peace, he could design one for the moon. The future seemed bright and easy. He felt sure Berlin's acceptance of his rocket would convince his father to let him be a scientist instead of a physician.

**CHAPTER 6** ♖ "Mankind will not remain on the Earth forever. At first he will timidly penetrate beyond the limits of atmosphere then finally conquer all space around the Sun."

**KONSTANTIN EDUARDOVITCH ZIOLKOVSKY**

# *Armistice, Marriage, and Study* [1918-1919]

B Y MARCH, 1918, Dr. Csallner was convinced that the rocket was the only and perhaps the last hope for a German victory. Defeat threatened like the mythical sword that hung by a single hair over the head of Damocles. The doctor realized it would not be easy to send Hermann's plans to military scientists in Berlin. The road to their Headquarters was paved with subordinate officers. After much pondering he thought of a shortcut, and sent for the young sergeant.

"Prepare to carry bacteria specimens to the hospital at Kronstadt."

Hermann's spirit sank. This had nothing to do with his missile. But the doctor was not finished.

"Tell the German Consul there to send your drawings

direct to Berlin. At once! If you have trouble with him send me a wire saying, 'Aunt Pepi terribly ill.' I'll understand and come to help you. Leave as soon as you can get ready!"

Though Kronstadt was only a few miles away, the train could not move fast enough to please the inventor sitting with his hands around a bulky roll of papers. In the city he left his suitcase at a hotel and went directly to the consulate. It was closed! There was nothing to do but deliver the specimens to the hospital and wait. All night he lay on his bed planning a speech to the Consul. He must explain his rocket in words which could be understood by a man ignorant of science. That would not be easy.

The next morning, when the Consulate opened, Hermann was at the door. After due formalities he was ushered into an imposing room. Behind an elegant desk sat the Consul, a man who gave the impression of being very important. He was puzzling over some papers before him. Finally he lifted his head and spoke, a degree of impatience in his tone.

"What can I do for you, Herr Oberth?"

The fateful moment had come. Hermann's breath was coming almost too rapidly to talk. Yet everything depended on the speech he had rehearsed. To break the sudden hush in the room he unrolled his papers. The sight of his rocket loosened his tongue and he began to talk, at first haltingly, then with ease. He explained the drawing of the fuel tank, the burning chamber, and the guiding rudders operated by a gyroscope, all so simple to him. The Consul shifted in his chair, obviously bewildered.

"Young man! Do you think this can win a war?"

"I beg you, Herr Consul, let Berlin decide."

The official arose. His voice had a tone of finality in it, yet was without either opposition or encouragement.

"I'll forward all this with my own papers." He moved

his hand to take in the documents. "It will take two weeks for a reply."

Hermann left the building, torn between hope and despair. If the military scientists really studied his design they were bound to be convinced that his rocket could cross the Channel. Just one dropped on Piccadilly Square might end the war.

After reporting to his own military hospital in Schaessburg, the young man groomed himself to call again on the blue-eyed girl whom he now called Tilly instead of her formal name, Mathilde. To his delight he found that she was interested in his rocket. That she might also be interested in him was more than he dared hope. The evening passed too swiftly and he departed, thinking that Tilly had more charm than any girl in the world. It seemed strange that he had known her so many years without discovering this. He wanted desperately to make her proud of him. Of course she would be the first to hear his good news from Berlin.

One week dragged by, or at least the days dragged. The evenings seemed to go by in a few seconds in the parlor at Tilly's home. Two weeks later there still was no report. Tilly insisted that this meant the German scientists were studying his rocket. Hermann did not voice his own fear that they had filed and forgotten it. With mounting anxiety he read the war bulletins, hoping for a hint of a proposed future weapon. But the papers overflowed only with accounts of American doughboys, who by April were swarming into France at the staggering rate of seventy-five thousand a week. There was also worse news: the Allies were moving forward against the weary Deutsche soldiers. The suspense of waiting robbed Hermann of his appetite and his sleep. Unless his rocket entered the war soon, it would be too late.

Although Dr. Csallner tried to raise the young inventor's spirits, his own heart held misgivings. The older man knew too well that it was common practice for the military to take what they could use wherever they found it. That was part of war rules.

Finally, an official letter came, with Hermann's documents. He checked to make sure everything had been returned. Not for an instant did he suspect that anything might have been copied. Relieved that none of his documents had fallen into the clutch of British sympathizers, he broke the official seal on the envelope and read the letter.

"We have carefully studied your sketches. Surely you know that rockets travel no farther than 7 kilometers [a kilometer is 0.62 miles], not hundreds. We are convinced that you have made a wrong calculation. Therefore we must reject your plan." *

Not one of Berlin's Crown Council suspected that they had seen plans for a weapon destined to shock the world a quarter of a century later. Had they rushed to manufacture it in 1918 the course of World War I might have been changed.

Hermann dreaded telling Tilly that Berlin did not want his plans. It took all the courage he could muster. He was encouraged when neither she nor her two sisters thought that Berlin's decision meant he was a failure. They all believed in him and in his rocket.

"Don't give up!" Tilly urged. "Some day the world will listen to you."

In July Hermann and Tilly walked down the church aisle to be married (Plate 2). Their honeymoon was short, since he had to return to his post of duty.

By August the German troops raced backward before the Allied Army. Realizing that victory had slipped from their grasp, the Deutsche generals boldly sent a command to the Kaiser.

---

* From *Hermann Oberth,* by Hans Hartl. Hannover: Theodore Opperman Verlag, 1958, p. 77.

"Open peace negotiations at once!"

Kaiser Wilhelm refused. Such talk was not for Prussians. He waited, hoping that those soldiers who had already won Iron Crosses for bravery would lead a forward charge. But by September the infantry had retreated to where it had begun at the Hindenburg Line, a defense built across northeastern France. Finally, in October, Germany appealed to President Wilson for an armistice.

"Unconditional surrender!" was the reply.

Then Hermann heard the worst: the German fleet had mutinied. The Allies were drawing together for a death blow, even threatening to bomb Berlin. In Transylvania, civilian tempers exploded. To the Saxons, Berlin was almost a sacred city. Moreover, they were weary of the strain of war. Almost every family had a chair left vacant by fighting; the Oberths had lost their son Adolf, Hermann's younger brother. Women were weak from lack of food. For years the population had endured meals of turnips: turnip bread, turnip soup, turnip coffee; they even smoked turnip cigarettes. Everywhere Hermann heard the same muttering: "Make the Kaiser give in!"

Hopefully the young couple followed the war dispatches. As soon as peace came Hermann could be discharged and they would have a real home together.

In the first week of November, delegates left the Crown Council to negotiate an armistice. Since they were in no position to haggle over terms, they listened, begging only for one concession, that German regiments be allowed to parade back home with flags flying and rifles in hand.

The Allies agreed. There seemed no need to humiliate an enemy, and, since he was being required to pay war indemnity, his pride and spirit should not be completely crushed.

On the eleventh hour of the eleventh day of the eleventh

month of 1918, World War I was officially over. In time
Hermann was discharged. Not only the town of Schaessburg, but all of Transylvania was in confusion. According
to the Treaty of Versailles, Austria-Hungary had vanished.
Transylvania had become part of Rumania (Plate 3). The
old flags were sadly hauled down. Natives went to their jobs
only to find foreign faces at their desks. Then an edict was
issued which literally left most Germans speechless. Only the
Rumanian language was to be spoken, no Deutsche.

Since Hermann did not know Rumanian he could not
get work. For a brief time he studied at the University of
Siebenbürgen, which by special permission was permitted
to teach in Hungarian, but at the end of the school year the
doors of the University closed. He returned to Schaessburg
to join Tilly and their new baby son, Julius. It was apparent
that the young father could not support a family by drawing
rockets. He needed a steady income, and to become a
teacher required more schooling. By this time Hermann's
father had agreed to the study of mathematics and physics
instead of medicine. In addition, the older man offered to
finance his son's advanced study.

Once again Hermann packed his luggage. This time he
put in not only his clothing but also his rocket designs,
which had become almost a part of him. He hoped that
at the University of Munich he could find a few spare
minutes to work on problems of outer space. He wanted
to study conditions beyond the atmosphere, to improve his
rocket pumps and steering device, and to invent some way
to keep his burning oven from melting in the high temperature of the gas.

For the safekeeping of his money, Tilly sewed six thousand lei, worth slightly less than a half-cent each, into his
straw hat. Both knew that his trip would be difficult, if not
dangerous. Public transportation had halted, and farmers'

carts were about the only vehicles on the roads. At places guards demanded identification from travelers, but Hermann assured his family that, being German, he would have no trouble crossing the border. Promising to send for Tilly and little Julius as soon as he found a house, he took his suitcases and set off for Munich.

**CHAPTER 7** ♜ "Enthusiasm and faith are necessary ingredients of every great project. Prophets have always been laughed at, deplored and opposed, but some prophets have proved to be following the true course of history."

WERNHER VON BRAUN

# "By Rocket to Interplanetary Space" [1919-1923]

THE SENTRY at the German border examined Hermann's passport and shook his head. It was against rules to admit a foreigner, especially an enemy Rumanian. Hermann bristled with arguments. Just because the Allies gave Transylvania to Rumania did not turn native Saxons into Rumanians. It was like claiming that a wave washing over an island made everyone a fish. Worn down with Hermann's words, the sentry wrote out a pass, which Hermann read in dismay. He could not manage a year's schooling on a visitor's permit. But since it was that or nothing, he accepted the paper and crossed the border.

On the way to Munich he saw that the old easy days of the Kaiser were gone. The country was now the Weimar Republic with a constitution and a Reichstag, or Congress. Everyone was grumbling over the war reparations laid on Germany. Military men muttered against the pitiful army and navy permitted Deutschland: only six battleships and one hundred thousand soldiers, practically nothing. Merchants complained that foreign trade had vanished; stores were closed and industries had collapsed. Veterans had no work and no pay. The value of money was sinking. Before the war an American dollar was worth four marks; now it bought nearly four trillion marks! When Hermann went to a postoffice to buy a stamp for a letter to Tilly he paid nearly a million marks for it. Also, he discovered that food was scarce and natives were loath to share their quota with strangers.

After arriving in Munich he could find no place to live. No one dared take in a foreigner. Rooms were registered and assigned only to Germans. In desperation he told his story to the police. They extended his pass and provided him with a small room.

"But you must move in six weeks!" they warned. "That's the law for foreigners."

Discouraged, he registered at the University. His spirits lifted when he learned he could take several classes in science. In a somewhat triumphant mood, he set out to see how the town had changed in his absence.

Instead of jolly burghers singing in beer gardens he found grim ex-soldiers in dingy halls. At one place a guttural-voiced veteran with an Austrian accent was giving a speech. Deutschland must unite under a powerful leader, he cried to his glum audience. And what better leader than himself,

Adolf Hitler! The German race had a mission as sacred as that of the Crusaders. In fact, the people were the new Crusaders. On them depended the salvation of the world, because Germans embodied true nobility and genius.

At the University Hermann learned that this man had organized his disgruntled following into what he called the National Socialist German Workers. Some students were impressed with the fellow's boldness, others were alarmed, but most were amused. This agitator was a comedian, a cheap copy of the Yankee funny-man, Charlie Chaplin, whose films were showing at the local cinema.

Hours of study helped drown Hermann's loneliness during the chilly autumn days. Rather than pack up every six weeks he moved to a nearby village and traveled each day by train. Christmas that year would have passed unnoticed but for a box of gifts. He had little time to get acquainted with other students; his mind was too much on his space craft. Neither did he notice another student at the University, a dwarfish fellow with sinister eyes. Hermann had no reason to suspect that this Joseph Goebbels would some day stand for evil, not only in his native land but throughout the world.

In March of the next year he transferred to Göttingen University, where he had heard that houses were plentiful. Tilly came to help find living quarters, but again the landlords gave the same reply: "Sorry, no foreigners." Back she went to Schaessburg and Hermann settled in a small room.

As the school year progressed, Hermann organized his work to have time for his rocket. The library offered no books on rocketry, nor could teachers guide him. He had to create outer-space science through study and his own thinking. Gradually he began to put his theory onto paper. To his delight, when he checked his figures they made sense. Then a new idea occurred to him: why not use this material as a thesis for his doctorate? It was original and based on scientific research. The more he pondered the idea, the better it appeared. Since he might be biased, he decided to reveal his secret to a professor for an impartial opinion. But Herr Dr. Ambronn gasped in consternation. He was no rocket man. Undaunted, Hermann knocked on the door of Herr Dr. E. Wiechert, the inventor of an early seismograph, and presented his documents. The scientist folded the pages with crushing words.

"I can't go aboard with you on this outer-space stuff. We will never escape the atmosphere."

The next day Hermann found a teacher of aerodynamics willing to glance at his papers. "Too many mistakes," was the verdict. Incredible as this seemed to Hermann, he determined to check again every figure. From the minute the library opened its doors until the closing bell he bent over books and manuscripts. His eyes ached from studying formulae and writing.

By the spring of 1921 he had designed a double rocket, the ancestor of the modern step-rocket. The two sections of the rocket were mounted in single file, the lower part to fall away after it had burned out. Fuel for the first stage was to be alcohol and oxygen; for the second, hydrogen and oxygen. On paper these appeared workable, but only testing would prove it.

All summer Hermann worked at the University. In the fall he transferred to Heidelberg University. Since its founding in the fourteenth century, it had collected rare manuscripts and books. He felt sure that among them he could find something to aid his search. The school had a reputation for both famous professors and alumni and he might meet men who talked the language of space. In addition, a doctorate from Heidelberg was a key to almost any college.

Again Tilly arrived and the couple hunted for a house.

No one wanted to rent to parents with two small children, and once more Hermann had to settle down alone. But now he had a definite goal, his degree, which gave purpose to his writing. Slowly his manuscript and drawings took shape. He labeled his rocket "Model B." It was to carry instruments to great heights and measure the temperature, density, and composition of upper atmosphere. The body measured 16 feet in length and weighed over half a ton. For its skin he recommended a lightweight metal, perhaps an aluminum alloy.

He worked constantly, designing even the smallest details. When he closed his eyes he could see the pumps pushing fuel into the burning oven to be vaporized and shot out as gas. Perhaps somewhere along that route he could use the cool liquids themselves to reduce the heat of the oven. Perhaps he could find a metal resistant to extremely high temperatures. Trials and errors were necessary to clear up mistakes. Because practical testing was needed, he gave no specific dimensions; his model was not intended as a blueprint for construction, but only to illustrate his theory. No doubt he would change it if he could borrow a laboratory and tools. Perhaps if he took a position with an airplane company he could use their equipment. As soon as he had his doctorate, this would be simple.

He tried to recall what he knew about planes, to be able to talk with a prospective employer. The Treaty of Versailles had forbidden Germany to build aircraft. By 1922 those of World War I were falling apart. Under pressure the Allies agreed to the construction of purely commercial planes. However, Deutsche factories did not understand the modern heavy craft. It was necessary for them to send aviation engineers to foreign lands to take special courses, and the Bolshevik government was strangely cooperative.

It was not long before a German airplane company

named Junkers became interested in a factory near Moscow.
When Russia offered tempting terms, the German government assisted Junkers by putting up a large sum of money.
The terms of the deal included the training of German
military pilots. Many German citizens felt apprehensive
about this, wondering whether the Prussian military spirit
was coming to life again. A factory just for commercial
planes would not have to be built so far from Allied inspec-
tion.

By working long hours Hermann was finally able to sub-
mit his thesis to the University. How proud Tilly was going
to be! Also, the title of Doctor would in a measure soften
his father's disappointment that his son was not a physician.

When the official letter came from the University of
Heidelberg, Hermann could hardly believe it. The University had refused him a degree. It could not have been
because of the material in his manuscript. Perhaps his writing had been poor. For expert opinion he asked the astronomer Professor Dr. Max Wolf to read it. Dr. Wolf's verdict
came in two weeks.

"Congratulations, young man. An excellent paper. Publish it!"

Hermann's spirit shot upward; a book to his name might
balance the lack of a doctorate. He mailed the sheaf of
papers to a scientific editor. The title would look exciting
in print, Die Rakete zu den Planetenräumen ("By Rocket
to Interplanetary Space").

While waiting for the publisher to send his acceptance
Hermann combed through periodicals to learn what others
were doing in rocketry, if anything. He found an item about
an American. Using the English taught him in German
schools, Hermann wrote to Dr. Robert H. Goddard, head
of the Physics Department at Clark University in Massa-
chusetts.

Dear Sir,

Already many years I work at the problem to pass over the atmosphere of our earth by means of a rocket. When I was now publishing the result of my examination and calculations I learned by the newspaper, that I am not alone in my inquiries and that you, dear Sir, have already done much important works at this sphere. In spite of my efforts, I did not succeed in getting your books about this subject.

Therefore I beg you, dear Sir, to let them have me. At once after coming out of my work I will be honored to send it to you, for I think that only by common work of the scholars of all nations can be solved this great problem.

> Yours very truly,
> Hermann Oberth
> Stud. Math. Heidelberg, Germany.*

Although the time of waiting was painful, the letter from the publisher finally arrived. Hermann tore open the envelope and began to read. The editor wrote that he dared not publish anything as fantastic as a book about a rocket for space travel lest his name lose its reputation among scientists.

Not wanting to confess to his family that he had failed again, Hermann sent the manuscript to another publisher, then another. Six times he received the same negative reply. At last he forced himself to face a hard fact. He was a failure: no doctorate and no book. Though Tilly would feel crushed with disappointment, he had to be honest with her. He dreaded to see her expression, but he packed his possessions and took the train for Schaessburg.

Arriving home, he blurted the tragic news in his usual forthright manner. Tilly received it in silence. After several moments she spoke, a challenge in her tone.

* Letter from the collection of Mrs. Robert H. Goddard.

"You can succeed without a doctorate."

This was encouragement enough. She was saying what Hermann secretly felt, that success depended on what he had in his head, not in his hand. He would become a greater scientist than some of those who had turned him down. Still, to gain a reputation as a space authority he needed to publish his theory. This was impossible when editors refused his manuscript.

"Publish it yourself!" said Tilly. Seeing he was astonished, she went on in calm tone. "I have saved ten thousand lei. Use that!"

Even with about fifty dollars down payment, it was not easy to find a publisher. After much letter-writing, the firm of R. Oldenbourg of Munich agreed to take a chance on what seemed like science-fiction. They planned to bring out a "paperback" of less than a hundred pages under Hermann's title, *Die Rakete zu den Planetenräumen*. The cover was to have no picture, only the title and author's name. Dubious as the publishers were about the success of the volume, they were totally unprepared for what happened.

**CHAPTER 8** ♖ "The time will come when a voyage into space will be a practical proposition."

HERMANN GANSWINDT

# A Best-Selling Book [1923-1927]

ONLY HERMANN and his family had faith in the book. In the writing he had made no effort to trick the reader into a fabulous yarn. Everything was based on scientific observations. Almost as if to discourage seekers of sensational stories, he had opened with four propositions and the blunt statement:

These I wish to prove in this book.

1. At the present level of science and technology it is possible to build machines which can climb higher than the earth's atmosphere.

2. With further improvements these machines can reach such speed that if left in space they will not fall back to the earth but will be able to resist the pull of gravity.

3. These machines can be built so that men can go up in them (probably without danger to their bodies).

4. It might be worthwhile to manufacture these ma-

chines when economic conditions improve, perhaps in a few decades.*

The balance of the book was divided into three sections. Part I was written to win engineers, astronomers, and scientists who wanted equations and formulae. Hermann discussed rockets and explained how they could travel faster than the speed of their own exhaust jet. He stated the possibility that a way could be found to use the rocket's own fuel to cool its burning oven, a process that was later adopted, after he had shown the way, and was called regenerative cooling.

Part II was devoted to his Model B. Many readers who studied this rocket assumed that the author was an expert in building such missiles. On the contrary, his designs came from his study of mathematics: he had no practical experience. In summing up this section he announced:

"I consider that in rocketry up to now there are two new essentials: the use of liquid fuel instead of the common explosives, and a two-stage or divided rocket. Both of these I have advanced." *

It was in Part III that he dared look into a fabulous future, and what he saw caught the interest of readers. He described a huge rocket, a Model E, which today would be called a spaceship. It would carry men to other worlds. The lack of the usual pressure or gravity would not be harmful, though it might produce a mental effect. The sensation of having no balance, or in modern terms, of being weightless, might cause a feeling of terror. This condition could also induce seasickness.

Of course there was danger in taking off from the earth, but not as much danger as might be imagined. Nor was

* *Die Rakete zu den Planetenräumen*, p. 7.
† *Die Rakete zu den Planetenräumen*, p. 68.

the return overly perilous, especially if landing on water. Moreover, the place for landing could be charted in advance.

Meteoroids, the countless particles of matter beyond the atmosphere were the ever-present peril to the traveler in space. However, large meteoroids were rare and a rocket ship might sail a hundred years without meeting one large enough to puncture a plate two centimeters thick.

A spaceship required a pilot and should be equipped with periscopes for him to observe the earth or other planets. To travel safely a man needed a special suit, and shoes with hooks that would grasp rungs on the ship's walls. The cabin would be equipped with tanks of liquid oxygen and nitrogen to renew the air.

The construction of spaceships, Hermann argued, would allow new kinds of experiments and provide new frontiers of knowledge. In a space rocket man could study the energy of short wavelengths of light, certain of which cannot be produced in a laboratory, yet are available in the blue and ultraviolet of the sky. Eventually a space vehicle could be guided around the moon to observe the unknown side.

Although the money needed to build such spaceships might at first glance appear enormous, it must be remembered that each one could be used for many trips, perhaps a hundred trips beyond the atmosphere and back. Hence the cost per unit would not be too great for the knowledge gained.

Certain rockets could remain in space and become little moons. (About forty years later these would be termed satellites.) Such orbiting moons could serve as communications stations, connecting places on the earth too far removed by the curvature of the earth to use straight-wave broadcasting.

Satellites would stand guard over icebergs and report their locations. Had there been such a sky sentinel on guard, the sinking of the *Titanic*, the famous passenger ship struck by an iceberg in 1912, would not have occurred. Future disasters at sea could be reported and victims rescued.

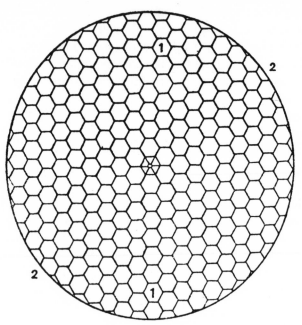

**Figure 1.** The space mirror. This design is similar to the one Oberth discusses in *Die Rakete zu den Planetenräumen*. (1) Wire meshwork; (2) external ring. [Figures 1–4 are taken from Oberth's book *Menschen im Weltraum* (Man Into Space).]

Another miracle of the future would be a space mirror. This, according to Hermann's design, was to consist of a metal frame over which thin metal foil was fastened. Since there is no wind to disturb it, the structure could be both light in weight and large in size. The mirror itself would consist of many small facets, each of which could be separately focused to throw light and heat from the sun onto any spot on the earth.

Such a mirror would have many uses. Towns could be lighted at night, icebergs melted from shipping lanes, and spring frosts warmed to save crops. Cyclones and tornadoes might be controlled. In areas of drought, an artificial depression might be created to bring rain. Thus weather to a degree could be regulated by man.

The use of a space mirror also has ominous aspects. In war, munitions factories or dumps could be blown up, grain fields withered, enemy towns set ablaze and marching troops scorched.

For such startling ideas as the above to win acceptance and get money from public funds, each project must either prove that it has an advantage or else become popular with the people. Hermann had small hope that his Model B would fulfill either of these requirements. Yet he believed in the principle behind it.

"I do not want to close this book without saying that the foregoing may all be built. But I will not claim that this will happen in the next ten years. . . ." *

While waiting for his book to appear, Hermann studied the Rumanian language and passed the teacher's examination. He received the title of Professor Secundar, qualifying him to teach high school, and was given a position in his home town of Schaessburg.

After several weeks, *Die Rakete zu den Planetenräumen* came from the press. Each afternoon after his classes Hermann searched through German periodicals for a review of the book. He felt sure that after it was read by government scientists, they would send for him. He imagined himself in a fine laboratory in Berlin, building his rocket for space exploration and travel.

* *Die Rakete zu den Planetenräumen*, p. 84.

But affairs in Germany were in turmoil. The ex-corporal Hitler had fired a revolver in a beer hall and proclaimed the end of the Weimar Republic. He was arrested immediately for inciting insurrection against the State, brought to trial and sentenced to five years in Landsberg Fortress.

Prison gave him time to write the book *Mein Kampf* ("My Struggle"). His followers argued loudly that Hitler's only crime was talking and that the Republic approved of free speech. As for his being dangerous to the State, he was merely an amateur painter. In passing weeks with prosperity flowing into the Rhineland, the prisoner was forgotten. Business picked up. Veterans went back to work. After thirteen months the comical ex-soldier was released.

Bewildered by the mass of political confusion, the German people sought escape. They decided there was no better route than by a flight into other worlds. In a few weeks the entire edition of *Die Rakete zu den Planetenräumen* had gone from bookshops into homes, and a flood of letters swamped the postoffice in Schaessburg. A young man named Wernher von Braun wrote that he could not understand the equations. A Berlin streetcar conductor begged for the privilege of placing the first human toe on the moon.

Young and old discussed the Professor's spaceship. Boys imagined themselves on the space station or in the rocket he had proposed to orbit around the earth. Girls dreamed of honeymooning at some celestial port. Men saw the sky depot as a place to study weather on the earth. Everybody tried to imagine themselves weightless and held down by the hooks of a space suit. Fantastic as these notions were, a professor had made them appear possible. His book was a relief from the grimness of war reparations and political intrigue. Orders for a second edition took the copies almost as they slid from the printing press.

Hermann was delighted. If word-of-mouth advertising carried his space theory to top officials, he would soon be building his rocket. Instead, his ideas reached the critics, who attacked them with venom. Who was this upstart who asserted that a rocket's fuel could be used to cool its own burning oven? Ridiculous! Firing a spaceship's fuel in an opposite direction to act as a brake? Absurd! It was all total nonsense.

Professors, physicists, and astronomers jumped into the debate. Their words carried weight. Hermann waited for some of them to defend his theory.

A Privy Councilor wrote in the *Journal of the Society of German Engineers:* "We believe that the time has not come for delving into such problems as these and probably never will come." A professor wrote in a distinguished review magazine, *Die Umschau:* "The author clearly has only a limited knowledge of equipment required for space experiments. . . . As to the possibility of taking this apparatus into spaces where there is no gravity and no air, it can only be said that the reactive driving power of a rocket depends on the presence of a mass of air. . . ."

Hermann begged for a few lines in magazines to reply to his critics. After numerous refusals, *Die Umschau* gave him space in their issue of March 22, 1924. After arguing his case he closed with these words:

"Of course there will be technical problems yet to solve in building a large rocket. But in the 17 years I have been working on them I have found nothing to prove that rocket manufacture is impossible or even doubtful. It can be done."

After moving to Mediasch (Plate 5), Hermann divided his time between classes and his family. But he could not forget rockets. Since his first book had brought him no laboratory or workshop in which he could build a rocket, he decided to try another book. This time he meant to appeal directly to the people, not to scientists who had ridiculed him. Perhaps the people would clamor for a rocket and thus make his ideas popular. With this hope he began to write *Wege zur Raumschiffahrt* ("The Road to Space Travel").

# CHAPTER 9  ♖  "The dream of yesterday is the hope of today and the reality of tomorrow."

**ROBERT H. GODDARD**

# *"The Girl in the Moon"*
# [1927-1929]

B y 1927 the space views planted by Hermann's first book were sprouting. In Berlin a group of enthusiasts formed a society which they called *Verein für Raumschiffahrt* (The Society for Space Navigation) or VfR. However, when the members tried to register the name, a German court objected. There was no such word as *Raumschiffahrt*. Such a false title was misleading.

With difficulty the organizers proved that new ideas bring new words into use and eventually into the dictionary. Finally permission was granted and the name registered. In English the name became The German Rocket Society. Within a year, the number of members had risen to 500. Hermann Oberth was among them. Now, more than ever, he longed to be in Berlin with men who talked his language of space.

Soon it appeared that everyone with a pen was writing about space travel. One of the most popular space writers in Germany was Willy Ley. In Russia, a deaf teacher,

Konstantin Ziolkovsky, was turning out magazine articles while Nikolai Rynin, a professor of Engineering at Leningrad had begun to publish his encyclopedic nine-volume work, *Interplanetary Travel*. It was not long before a leading German film company Universum-Film-Aktiengesellschaft (Universal Film Corporation), or UFA, decided that a rocket would be a fine vehicle on which to ride to the bank with bags of marks. When it was announced that the famous director, Fritz Lang, would head the production, success was certain.

A script was written using Hermann's book as a foundation. The film title was *Frau im Mond* ("The Girl in the Moon"). Sets were designed and actors chosen. Giant backdrops were painted showing jagged mountains against a starry sky. Then Professor Oberth was invited to be the technical advisor.

This was exactly to Hermann's liking. Obtaining a leave of absence from his school, he took the train to Berlin. While the wheels rattled under him he studied the passing countryside. Of course, all the towns now bustled with prosperity. Gone were the unemployed veterans, and nowhere was the least hint of a coming great depression. Occasionally, in some depot he saw men greet each other with a strange salute, and the words "Heil Hitler." It was no secret that the organizer of the Nazi Party had borrowed his salute from Mussolini.

Nearing Berlin, Hermann saw men in brown shirts whom he identified from pictures as members of the S.A. Troops, also known as the *Sturmabteilung*, or Storm Troopers. In the depot he found men in black shirts. These belonged to the S.S. Troops or *Schutz Staffel*, the Elite Guard, who were feared as much as the Storm Troopers.

Leaving his baggage at a hotel, Hermann hurried to the home of Fritz Lang. Autumn leaves were falling along the streets of Germany's most famous city. He was excited by the thought that a movie about a trip to the moon would spread knowledge of his rocket. Then the government was bound to realize its possibilities.

Over coffee and cakes the Professor and the movie director discussed the film. Hermann was alarmed when he learned it was to be the adventure of six persons landing on the moon.

"But, Herr Lang, there's no air on the moon so how can—?"

"Well, put some there!" came the reply.

Hermann scowled. As a scientist with a reputation for honesty, could he accept such distortions? Before he could protest Lang was showing sketches for the moon: rolling ground like snowdrifts, mountains like church spires, and a sky lighted by millions of stars.

"Don't complain, Professor!" Lang waved his guest silent. "We can do *anything* with poetic license."

Hermann left with a confusion of emotions. Lang did not want him to act as technical advisor. He wanted only the name of Oberth to give his film a flavor of authenticity. Hermann was about to resign when he remembered that the UFA had promised him a laboratory, a workshop, and helpers. After he had built a small rocket model for trick photography in the movie, why not build a real one? Willy Ley was trying to convince the company of the value of firing a genuine rocket as publicity on the day of the première.

So delighted was The German Rocket Society to have the author of space travel in their midst, they elected him their president. Accepting the honor, he tried to hide his nervousness. As yet he had built a rocket only on paper. He was not an engineer, not even a mechanic accustomed to tools.

Winter and summer drifted by. The school at Mediasch

gave him another leave of absence. That autumn he was still working in the rickety shed of the UFA, but he did not mind. At last he was building a real rocket, his own invention (Plate 6). In another building a metal worker was shaping a six-foot aluminum torpedo to house the motor. On the day of the première, his rocket would be launched with fanfare, bands, and publicity. Others might copy it, but he had shown the way to space travel. He must not fail this time.

After many changes of plan, Hermann settled on a steel motor with copper lining. Because of its cone-shape, it acquired the name of *Kegelduese* ("cone-nozzle"). The upper pointed section was bolted to the lower nozzle part. The whole apparatus consisted of a vacuum-insulated dewar flask for liquid oxygen, a bottle of nitrogen, and a tank of gasoline. Copper tubing connected the oxygen and gasoline to the motor.

Nobody worried that the liquids were dangerous to use or that the motor was difficult to start. The only way to ignite the fuel was by direct flame, for safety a burning rag on the end of a long stick.

In the spring of 1929, Hermann received notice that he had been awarded the first REP-Hirsch Prize for his book *Wege zur Raumschiffahrt*. This prize, established by the Frenchmen Robert Esnault-Pelterie and André Hirsch, was awarded each year to the person who had done the most for space travel. Furthermore, because Hermann's book was so vital, the prize money had been doubled to ten thousand francs, about four hundred dollars. Not accustomed to such good fortune, he telephoned Willy Ley.

"Is this a joke?" asked the modest Hermann.

Assured that it was real, he started to work with fresh enthusiasm. Though the UFA had gone back on its promise to supply material for his rocket, he now had the money to buy what he needed.

Since trick photography was necessary in making the film, he constructed a small wooden model similar to his large rocket. The miniature was photographed as being launched toward the moon, with thousands watching. Actually, the launching pad was a tabletop and the crowd composed of pins. Cigar smoke provided the fog, while a fine wire drew the model toward a starry sky. Later, the jet flame was added by covering the nozzle of a blowtorch with the model and swinging the two to simulate a take-off. When Hermann saw the result thrown on a screen, he caught his breath. It appeared genuine. He wondered if his real rocket would behave as well.

It came as a shock when the company announced October 15th as the date of the première. There was still much to be done on the rocket to prepare it for launching. He tried to speed up his work, putting in longer hours. Repeatedly there were setbacks: breakages, changes in design, lack of material or experienced helpers. Furthermore, the police tormented him by regularly checking his supply of gasoline and liquid oxygen. Because he was not a citizen and had failed to acquire the proper license, the law allowed him only two liters, about two quarts, not enough for testing.

Far into the night Hermann lingered over desk or workbench. He tried to ignore his exhaustion. Then the catastrophe the police had tried to prevent happened: explosion. His eyes and hearing were slightly damaged, and he was badly shaken.

Persistence drove him back to his shop after only a week. The day for launching the rocket was approaching and the rocket was not ready. UFA was beating its advertising drums, exciting all Berlin. Success at the launching could mean capturing the attention of the German Government with its limitless funds for rocketry. Yet every evening, when

Hermann took inventory of his progress, failure appeared almost certain.

In desperation he accepted volunteer workers. Willy Ley recruited a fair-haired boy of about seventeen years. Although he was the son of a former Minister of Agriculture and was expected to manage his father's rich lands, Wernher von Braun had visions of flying to Mars and Venus.

"Herr Professor," said Wernher, "though I'm still in school I'd like to work for you in my spare hours."

Hermann accepted the boy, never suspecting that his pupil was destined to guide America in the dash into space.

Though the night of October 15th turned cold and wet, the elite of Germany came out for the most elegant première Berlin had ever seen. Big Mercedes sedans drew up to unload top hats and sables onto the carpeted marquee. Cameras clicked, jewels sparkled, spectators jostled under umbrellas. Nobody gave a second glance to the gaunt figure of a tired man with sad eyes. He slipped into the theater without fanfare, and from a cheap seat watched the first rocket roar off into outer space, his little wooden model.

Everybody was happy about *Frau im Mond* except Hermann, whose real rocket had never left the ground. There had not been time to test the fuels. To satisfy public questioning, the UFA announced that weather prevented the launching. Only Hermann and The German Rocket Society knew the heartbreaking facts. The problem arose of what to do with the partially finished rocket.

"Sell it," said Hermann, "and use the money to build a bigger one."

"Give it to a museum," argued Willy Ley.

Since nobody could agree, the rocket stood around for years, until finally it disappeared. Some say it went to a dusty corner, others that it was sold for scrap.

Bitter and without funds, Hermann returned to Tilly

and his four children. He wanted to get acquainted with his new baby son, Adolf. As the coach chugged through the vineyards near Mediasch, he came to a conclusion: he was a failure. He must settle down and forget rockets. They could not provide him with a living. He was only a mathematician, not a scientist. The only tools he knew were logarithms, equations, and formulae. He would be just a good teacher, father, and husband. That was his fate.

**CHAPTER 10** ♖ "To conquer space would be an achievement surpassing anything that man has yet accomplished; the greater, therefore, the challenge."

HAROLD SPENCER JONES

# An Invitation to Build Rockets [1930-1932]

B Y THE TIME the train pulled into Mediasch, Hermann was planning to work in the student metal shop in his spare time. This would give him the opportunity to use tools and experiment with rocket parts. Moreover, here he could buy pure methane, or marsh gas, to use instead of gasoline, and perhaps even find time in which to study conditions beyond the earth's atmosphere.

But he was not allowed to work serenely in his academic ivory tower. The publicity of the REP-Hirsch Prize put his name into discussion. More critics flayed him. Some churchmen claimed that by soaring into space man was assaulting the gates of Heaven. It was sacrilegious! Furthermore, it was suicidal. If a spaceship was not riddled by meteoroids, the passengers would be killed by the fierce rays from the sun or the Northern Lights.

Hermann did not waste energy by answering. No one had a road map to Heaven. As for meteoroids hitting a spaceship, nobody would know that answer until man went into space to learn the facts. It was known that whenever a particle of stone or metal entered the earth's atmosphere, friction turned it into a shooting star. Probably none of these pieces were larger than a golf ball and most of them were finer than grains of sand. To learn their size man had to go to where they were, which meant riding in rockets or spaceships. As for the danger of cosmic rays, science knew neither their origin nor nature. The rays might be continuously penetrating everything on the earth.

By the end of the school year, the lure of the rocket had proved too strong to resist and Hermann was again in Berlin trying to raise funds for research. But money was hard to acquire. The Great Depression had leaped the ocean from the crash on America's Wall Street and in Germany unemployment was increasing. One man, guided by astrology, claimed to know the solution. He appeared at important Nazi meetings crying that Deutschland would find prosperity only by driving back what he called the "Red Tide" of Bolshevism. To none but his intimates did he add, "and by extermination of the Jews." Hungry audiences ate these crumbs of propaganda served by a little man, Joseph Goebbels.

While Hermann and his former assistant, Rudolf Nebel, went from one foundation to another asking for research money, an accident occurred which perhaps changed the course of history. A rocket enthusiast, Max Valier, was killed while experimenting with a rocket to run his automobile. A cry arose: "Outlaw the rocket!" In time the public forgot the affair, with the exception of one man. Hitler remembered the death of his friend and turned against rocketry, a prejudice that was to influence his decrees in World War II.

Day after day Hermann heard the same negative reply to his request. Finally he approached the Director of the least likely institution of all, the *Chemisch-Technische Reichsanstalt* ("Government Institute for Chemistry and Technology"). Dr. Ritter listened to Hermann, looked over his drawing of the *Kegelduese* and then gave his verdict. Though he had no money to donate for research, if Professor Oberth could demonstrate his liquid-fuel rocket motor, the Institute would give him a certificate to aid in soliciting funds.

This was the most encouragement Hermann had received. The motor to be demonstrated was the one he had designed while working on the *Frau im Mond* movie. The German Rocket Society was delighted at the prospect. Three members volunteered to help: Wernher von Braun, Rudolf Nebel, and an engineer, Klaus Riedel. After checking every part of the *Kegelduese* they sent notice to Dr. Ritter that the motor was ready to show what it could do.

The test took place in the woods on the outskirts of Spandau, a suburb of Berlin, near a shack which offered a degree of protection from possible explosion. Clouds hung over the treetops and everything was damp from rain. Because liquid oxygen has a temperature of minus 298 degrees Fahrenheit, it transformed all moisture into ice crystals, coating valves, pipes, and even the gloves of the men with white frost. Dr. Ritter and Hermann waited, the one curious, the other anxious. While the propellants were being turned on by one helper, another stood behind a shelter and stretched out his arm to apply a burning rag on the end of a pole to the gas-spitting engine. The motor started with a deafening roar. Hermann was overjoyed; his rocket had not failed him. Returning to his office, Dr. Ritter wrote a statement that the *Kegelduese* "had performed without mishap on July 23, 1930, for 90 seconds, consuming 6 kilograms of liquid oxygen and 1 kilogram of gasoline, and delivering a constant thrust of about 7 kilograms [15 pounds]." *

When Hermann showed this certificate to The German Rocket Society, plans were made to find a permanent laboratory. With nine hundred members all soliciting donations from manufacturers, their workshop would be stocked with lathes, drill presses, and other tools. A man was appointed to hunt for a testing field which was to bear the sign *Raketenflugplatz* ("Rocket Airdrome"), the first in the world.

Hermann wrote Tilly the good news that at last he could devote full time to research. His moonship was almost a reality. Then he received a letter from his school at Mediasch. The officials were sorry, but they could not extend his leave of absence. Unless he returned his place would be filled.

Once again Hermann had to postpone his deepest wish. His wife and children depended on him. Rocket research offered a nebulous income, he knew, and a teacher's pay was steady. There was no choice. He put away his certificate and took a train for home.

Although he returned bodily to the classroom, his mind could not stay away from space travel. In a lecture in Vienna he predicted rocket travel from that city to New York in less than an hour. He urged governments to plan for mail service between the continents. These mail rockets would have no crew, would carry about seventy pounds of cargo,

* From *Rockets, Missiles and Space Travel,* by Willy Ley. New York: Viking Press Inc., 1961, p. 134.

and fly at a height of about seventy-five miles. He also prophesied that passengers could fly in comfort if their cabin was kept level by use of a gyroscope (for a similar craft see Plate 7).

Between preparing lessons for his students and working on his rocket designs he read the German papers, hoping for news of the Rocket Society. But the big news was the election that had swept the Nazis into power on the slogan, "Stop the Red Tide!" Their propaganda had filled the voters with fear of the Bolsheviks; only after his Party had won did Hitler make public his other hatred. The new members of the Reichstag, Germany's legislative assembly, arrived for the first session wearing brown shirts and shouting, "Germany awake! Judea perish!"

Torn between his longing to be in Berlin, building rockets, and his relief to be out of Germany, Hermann continued to watch for news of the Rocket Society. Most of the print concerned the Great Depression. Food was scarce and cameras were *verboten* at banquets of the Nazi lords. Although the "Old Gentleman," Field Marshal von Hindenburg remained president of the Weimar Republic, Hitler was maneuvering for control. He promised all things, even the restoration of the monarchy. His private army, the Storm Troopers, boldly appeared everywhere in their brown shirts, wide brown pants, leather belts, and boots. Though trained as military men they were placed in social and political positions to spy for their Chief, their very presence producing an awe akin to fear. By night Hitler's "Painting Squads" daubed swastikas on streets and buildings to imply that the whole capital was turning to him as their champion against the Reds.

Hermann viewed with alarm the news that art collectors were sending their best canvases "on loan" to foreign countries. Ernst Lubitsch, the noted movie director, migrated to the United States with the announcement: "Nothing good is going to happen here for a long time." There were hints that Hitler intended to abolish the Versailles Treaty, but that was too fantastic to believe. The Allies of World War I would never permit it. As for his hating the Jews, that must be false, since the papers pointed out that Dr. Albert Einstein was often invited to his social functions.

Hermann was puzzled. Were the Reds as dangerous as the propaganda proclaimed? He had not long to wait for the answer. On a snowy afternoon his doorbell rang. From his study he heard the maid answer. Presently she appeared at his doorway and whispered that a man wanted to see him but refused to give his name. Hermann thought the visitor might be from The German Rocket Society. Since Rumania and Germany were not on friendly terms, a traveler might prefer not to use a German name.

"Show him in," Hermann said, shoving his papers into a drawer.

The man who entered was a shabbily dressed stranger, with a fierce glint in his eyes. In broken German he ordered the window shades closed. Trapped, Hermann obeyed. When he returned to his desk the visitor moved near and lowered his voice.

"Herr Professor, I come to talk to you on an important matter. I'm sure you will not reveal my visit. You're wise enough to know that talk is dangerous."

With assurance, the guest sat down and leaned forward, his mouth close to Hermann's ear.

"I come from the Soviet Union to ask if you are ready to work for us. We know all about you. We have your drawings."

Hermann stared at the man. Was this a trick of the Rumanian security police? Perhaps they had opened his letters to Berlin telling about rockets or had read mail coming to him that mentioned the Reds in Germany. Not daring to take chances, he spoke sternly.

"Let me see your passport or identification!"

"Ha! A Russian passport in Rumania would send me to jail. I came 'black' across the border; you know, illegally. But I've got identification of the best kind." From a pocket he drew wads of money and tossed them onto the desk. "There! Ten thousand lei to start. We'll pay you three thousand rubles a month and provide everything you need: laboratory, house, cigars, liquor. No tax! All free! What do you say, Professor?"

Hermann stared at the man and at the money. Here was an offer to fulfill his life's dream of working out his ideas in a laboratory without any financial worries.

"What would I work on for the Soviets?"

"On what you like most, rockets."

"As war weapons?"

"Well, now, Professor, my country wants to give a scientist like you the chance he deserves. Of course we don't want war. But if we're forced to defend socialism against capitalism, that's a different story. Naturally, we'd use rockets."

Hermann tried to hold his voice to a deadly calm.

"Does Russia know how to build rockets?"

"Show me one of your latest drawings!" challenged the guest. "I'll add to it."

From his desk drawer Hermann lifted an incomplete sketch of a steering device with which he had been having trouble. The Communist studied it a moment, took a pencil and added a few lines as though from memory. Hermann blinked in consternation. One lever had solved the problem, yet he had not been able to think of it. This man was no fool. It was evident that Russia was far advanced in rocketry. After a tense moment, the visitor lighted a match and burned the paper with the drawing.

"Now, Professor, what do you say?" He pushed forward the money.

Hermann folded his arms. "No! Thank you."

The man gathered the lei. "I'll be back." He arose, moved to the door, and said, "Remember you are a father. We have eyes and ears everywhere. Yes, *everywhere!*"

After the Communist had gone, Hermann locked the front door. The wet shoeprints on the floor proved he had not been dreaming. It was all too apparent that Russia was producing rockets for war. He must alert Berlin at once. Taking pen and paper, he began to write.*

* This meeting and conversation has been condensed from *Hermann Oberth*, by Hans Hartl. Hannover: Theodore Oppermann Verlag, 1958, pp. 157 ff.

# CHAPTER 11 ♜ "Man himself is the only ultimate force for good or evil."

WERNHER VON BRAUN

# *Germany Arms Itself* [1933-1936]

I T DID NOT TAKE military authorities long to answer Hermann's letter. Though they begged him not to go to the Soviet Union, there was no word or hint about going to Berlin. Hermann folded the letter, thinking it was odd that Germany did not realize the danger from Russia. Possibly the Rocket Society was secretly working on weapons for defense. If only he knew what the members were doing!

Hoping to find that information, he thumbed through magazines after his classes and learned that the Society now had its own headquarters and a testing field. Although the workshop was an old warehouse, it was equipped with power machines, tools, and also many helpers. Unemployed draftsmen, electricians, and metal workers were glad to trade their labor for free living quarters in some of the other buildings. It was a busy place. Already Willy Ley and an engineer had built the first rocket.

For days Hermann pondered the strange fate which prevented him from building rockets. Surely his whole life would not be spent designing them for other hands to put together. While he was trying to find a way to change his apparent fate the political situation suddenly changed. Hitler had become Chancellor of Germany, and the Nazi Army paraded with torches and bayonets in a display of power. They even had a password to identify Party members to each other: "Grandmother is dead."

With apprehension, Hermann wondered if this change in government would affect the development of rockets. He had not long to wait for the answer. "By Order of *der Fuehrer*" the Army Ordnance was to take charge of rocket engineering. Rockets would be built solely for "national defense" and no private group would be permitted to experiment on them outside State supervision. All plans for space flight were to be abandoned. Hermann knew if he had stayed in Berlin his chances for working on his space ideas would be less than in Mediasch. Now young von Braun must quit his dream of reaching Mars and Venus.

Before many weeks The German Rocket Society began to shrivel. Members could not pay their dues because "all money belonged to *der Fuehrer* and what was not needed for food should be donated to the Party." Men who wanted to work on rockets joined the group of Captain Walter Dornberger at the government experimental station in Kummersdorf near Berlin. Others, such as Willy Ley, prepared to close their business affairs and migrate to the United States.

Passing months brought no encouraging news. Chancellor Hitler, publicized as the hard-working father to his people, rode in a car with a bullet-proof windshield and was preceded and followed by armed bodyguards in open Mercedes sedans. Did he fear internal trouble? To make sure that the

Nazis held control he created a force of secret state police called *Geheime Staatspolizei,* a name soon shortened to Gestapo. These men penetrated every strata of society to ferret out possible traitors. A citizen could be arrested for failing to give the "Heil" salute: the maximum punishment was death. Often the accused had no chance to defend himself. Every citizen lived in fear of a rap on his door in the middle of the night.

By Christmas the Chancellor was pictured as a "savior with a sword." In art galleries "undesirable" paintings gave place to pictures of Hitler, his favorite "The Standard Bearer," showing him in shiny armor astride a white charger. The Propaganda Ministry, under the direction of Joseph Goebbels, ordered all statues of Jews removed from churches. This was shocking to Hermann. Surely the order did not mean Jesus or Mary. Few citizens dared protest, in fear of the Gestapo. Holiday decorations showed old Santa wearing the uniform of a Storm Trooper giving the Heil salute.

Gradually Hermann saw how his family would fare in the Fatherland. If he wanted to take them to a funny movie, he would discover that Charlie Chaplin films had been banned as poking ridicule at *der Fuehrer's* moustache. At the opera house, music by Jewish composers was *verboten!* If Tilly grew weary of cabbage, potatoes, margarine, and rye bread, she could feast on the motto "Guns Before Butter." In the stores she would find no more French fashions. Their children would also have their lives changed. The oldest daughter, Erna, would have to wear "Gretchen" braids, flat heels, black skirts of ankle length, and brown jackets bearing the swastika. Since she was nearly fourteen, she would soon be registered in the Hitler Maidens group to do half a year's work, free, for the State. Little Ilse would also be trained in the Young Maidens. Their son Julius would be enrolled in the Hitler Youth. Surely so much regimentation was not necessary to stop the Red Tide, Hermann thought. Was it possible *der Fuehrer* had other ambitions?

The last question occurred again when Hermann learned about the German air force. Commercial planes were being equipped with observers shelters, or nacelles, perched on top like bird nests. Bomb bays and machine guns to fire through window frames had been added. Officially they were listed not as war planes but as "multi-purpose craft." The Professor had no way of suspecting that the new Luftwaffe was on its way to becoming the terror of Europe, or that it would ever touch his life.

Another blow to Hermann's feeling of security was a second offer to build rockets for a foreign country, this time Japan. At once he refused. Unless the Fatherland awakened to the need for defense it might be too late. The only defense from one rocket was another, more powerful and with longer range.

Hermann's hope for the safety of Germany rose when he learned that Major Dornberger had built a rocket with a thrust of 660 pounds and was aiming for the fantastic thrust of 2,000 pounds. Then came news that the Deutsche Ordnance was scouting for a testing field far from civilization, perhaps near the coast where rockets could be fired over the water. Hermann recalled a place near the Baltic Sea where his rocket for *Frau im Mond* was to have been fired. No doubt Wernher von Braun had already suggested that section to authorities. He and his father formerly went hunting in the woods of Peenemünde.

Whenever Hermann thought of German rockets he wondered why the government did not send for him. Those the military was building were based on his discoveries, on his designs, on all he had revealed in his books. Headquarters might even be using the documents he had submitted during World War I. He was sure that some day he would be invited to join the rocket group. In the meantime, he would keep making improvements in order to be ready with suggestions when his great chance came.

One day while he was studying, a letter came from the royal office in Bucharest. Hermann was surprised and apprehensive. King Carol of Rumania did not write a teacher without strong reason. He opened the envelope and read a brief note.

> His Majesty grants an audience to Professor Hermann Oberth on Friday, April 22, 1935, at 5:00 P.M. in the afternoon at the castle in Bucharest. His Majesty wishes to learn about rocket progress. Time for the audience, 25 minutes. Proper attire: black jacket and needle-striped trousers.*

The whole family was in a flurry to get him off at the depot. Arriving at a Bucharest hotel, Hermann telephoned the castle as he had been instructed by letter. A coach bearing the Royal Crown soon pulled up in front of the lobby door and a liveried coachman escorted him outside. Police whistled at other vehicles to halt while the State coach traveled down the street.

At the palace, Hermann felt sure he was again a part of some Jules Verne tale. Uniformed guards ushered him along plush halls and into a small study lined with books. Behind a desk sat a man who looked up with a cordial smile.

"Sit down, Professor," said King Carol, extending his

* From *Hermann Oberth*, by Hans Hartl. Hannover: Theodor Oppermann Verlag, 1958, p. 164.

hand. After a few casual remarks he launched into a discussion of rocketry.

Hermann hesitated to reply. Should he talk in simple terms as to a child? A monarch was not expected to keep abreast of science.

"Talk to me as to an engineer," said the King, as if reading the question in his guest's mind.

This remark opened the door to a steady flow of words and queries that continued past the allotted time. Finally the King straightened.

"Professor, will you build a rocket institution for Rumania? You will have government financing."

Again Hermann stood at a crossroad. To refuse the King of the land where he lived was not easy, and it meant turning down an offer of a laboratory for his research. Still, he was a Saxon by birth and every ounce of his loyalty was to his Deutschland, not to Rumania. It was not right to sell his knowledge to a former enemy of Germany. He must be true to his own integrity, though he remained poor and unknown. Tilly and his parents would want it that way. He took a deep breath and pulled up his shoulders.

"Forgive me, Your Majesty. I have no talent for organization. Permit me to work in Mediasch."

Without offense, the King arose to signify that the interview had ended. When he pressed a button a uniformed escort appeared. Royalty and science parted.

All the way home on the train Hermann was troubled with doubts. He had now turned down Russia, Japan, and Rumania while waiting for a call from his Fatherland, a call which might never come.

The next day he wrote to Berlin. In blunt words he reminded them that foreign countries were on the trail of rockets. A race into space had begun. Who knew whether this would lead to space travel or to war with space weapons? After a brief hesitation, Hermann went on. If the men at Kummersdorf and at Peenemünde were still following his earlier designs, they were out of date. He had improved those models. Could he come and discuss this with them?

After posting the letter he tried to concentrate on preparing lessons for his students. Worried that he had been too bold in his letter, he watched the mails, but nothing came from Berlin. When he had almost given up hope, he received Official callers, several German officers who wanted to know what he had in mind for the defense of the Fatherland.

Hermann explained an anti-aircraft missile he had invented, a rocket using a solid propellant that cost about one cent per pound. The propellant was cheap and readily available because it was made synthetically from coal, water, and air. He knew how to compound this substance. As for the rocket's flight, the first part would be controlled by radio. Then, when nearing its target, a "homing" device took over. He would go into further details in Berlin.

When he was finished, the officer in command said, "Thank you very much, Herr Professor. You'll hear from us."

With that they left. For months he heard nothing. By the early part of 1936, Hermann realized that a new world was in the making. England had a new ruler, Edward VIII. Russia boasted that their great rocket expert, Ziolkovsky, had willed his writings to "the Bolshevik Party and the Soviet Government, the leaders of human cultural progress." Nobody knew what startling inventions his papers might contain. From America came reports that Dr. Robert H. Goddard had sent a rocket up to the astounding height of 7,500 feet. It appeared that Germany was being encircled by rockets, and Hitler was depending only on his Luftwaffe to meet them. Perhaps the experiments at Peenemünde would convince him of the value of rockets for defense.

# CHAPTER 12 ♜ "Knowledge is tomorrow's most important tool."

KRAFFT A. EHRICKE

# World War II [1937-1941]

I N THE SPRING of 1937, Hermann received a long-awaited letter from the Reich Air Ministry. His whole family was excited by the news that Hermann was to be "built into the system." It was mutually agreed that Tilly and the children would remain in Mediasch until he found a house for them in Berlin, and amidst waving of arms and happy voices he hurried to catch the next train.

Arriving at the German capital, he met representatives of the air force and army, including Major Dr. Dornberger and Dr. von Braun. The men gathered around a table in a private room, where drawings and documents were spread out. Hermann noticed a startling resemblance to those he had submitted long ago. All morning he answered their questions as best he could. In the afternoon Dr. Dornberger arose and folded the plans.

"Stay where you can be reached, Herr Professor," he said.

"But I came here to work on rockets."

"Not yet. We'll let you know. Good day."

86

Back to Mediasch went the discouraged teacher. The men from the Peenemünde experimental station had wanted only information from him. He might never hear from them again. During the following months he found no mention of rocket news in German periodicals. Instead he learned that food was getting so scarce in Germany that people sent butter as a gift with a note: "Fatty regards." Letters from friends reported that at Chancellery parties Storm Troopers and Elite Guards disguised themselves as footmen to guard *der Fuehrer*, an indication that perhaps Hitler feared civil war. There was little alarm over foreign entanglements, since everybody remembered the horrors of World War I and rebelled at the thought of fighting again.

A year later a letter came that both pleased and disappointed Hermann. He was asked to join a rocket program at the Technical College in Vienna. Though this was not Berlin, it was at least in Austria, a part of what was then called Greater Germany. Also, it offered an opportunity to work in a well-equipped laboratory at a fabulous salary. Without hesitation, he once again packed his suitcase.

Arriving at the College, he discovered that he was substituting for another professor in a newly created job. Nobody knew exactly what he was expected to do. When he wrote to the Air Experimental Station to ask for his assignment, the reply was even more baffling. In substance it said: "Do whatever you want but keep Professor Busemann informed." Professor Adolf Busemann was one of the leading scientists at the German Academy for Aerodynamic Research.

Hermann was annoyed. It was impossible to carry on the government's research without knowing how far Peenemünde had progressed. He might duplicate their output. Was he being employed merely to hold him available for questioning? he wondered. Even if he were, here was the opportunity he had always wanted: tools, machinery, an income, and freedom to follow his own research. His indignation melted into optimism. He would continue on his own rocket problems: the development of his anti-aircraft rocket which he had already revealed to the military, the best combustion for alcohol and liquid air, and the best means for creating pressure in a rocket tank. With his usual concentration, he set to work.

By the time he was deep in his project, he was ordered to the Technical College in Dresden. He protested in vain. The reply was firm and explicit. He was to research fuel pumps for the A-4 rocket, later to be called the V-2. With no alternative, he abandoned his work and took the train.

Trying to ease his disappointment with the assurance that at last he was to work on further improvement for the rocket he had originally designed, he went to his laboratory in Dresden. He felt handicapped by not having an actual rocket in the laboratory but after many days of work, he had perfected a pump design and submitted it to authorities. To his consternation he was informed that an engineer at Peenemünde had designed a similar one. Unable to contain his anger, Hermann accosted the top officials.

"Again you have pushed me onto a dead-end rail," he blurted, making no effort to conceal his feelings. "Now I'm through. I'm going back to Mediasch. Good-by, gentlemen!"

"Ahhh, Herr Professor, that is *verboten* for you. You know too much to leave Germany."

"Then send me to work at Peenemünde!"

"Impossible! That is top-secret. You are a Rumanian."

Hermann strode from the office straight to the State police. His identification satisfied them and he was given proof of his German citizenship. He returned to slap the document onto the military desk. As usual it was put on file and he was told, "We'll call you."

Tilly's arrival in Dresden with the family eased the misery of waiting. It was shocking to realize that his children were growing up. Julius was a handsome youth of twenty. Erna and Ilse were teenagers eager to assume the role of young ladies, and young Adolf, his baby, played at war with marching and wooden guns. Fear tightened around the father's heart at this reminder of the military. Would it call his two sons for training? Though he was sure history would not repeat itself he read the papers with mounting apprehension.

By 1939 Hitler was shuttling his fighter squadrons from city to city. Former opposition to his war games appeared to have melted and he was proclaimed the bloodless conqueror. Had he not brought the Sudetenland Germans into the Reich without battle? They lived in that part of Czechoslovakia bordering Germany. This proved he would not start a war. Neither would England, being in no condition to fight. *Der Fuehrer* had announced that "Britain must recognize her militarily hopeless position." The Russians were not potential enemies, because the German Chancellor and Stalin had shaken hands in peace and friendship. The talk of war could not be serious.

But on the first of September, 1939, world peace ended. It was a humid morning and the Kroll Opera House was packed with uniforms. *Der Fuehrer's* voice rose to dramatic heights. Despite his warnings, the Poles had attacked the Reich. They would not listen to his words. He had no choice. He was forced to speak to them in the language they asked for: war!

When the message flashed over the air waves to Dresden, Hermann and Tilly shuddered. Their son Julius might be summoned for active duty unless the Regular Army could end this petty conflict. No doubt victory would come swiftly. The Chancellor sounded optimistic.

"I desire nothing other than to be the first soldier of the German Reich. I have again put on that old coat which was the most sacred and the most dear to me of all. I will not take it off until the victory is ours—or I shall not live to see that end." *

When France and England declared war on Germany, it came as a surprise to Hermann. He had been led to believe that the other countries were too weak to fight.

At his laboratory he noticed the tense faces of his fellow scientists. They assured each other that the war could be nothing more than a swift nightmare, since there was no indication that the army meant to fire the big guns which their engineers had installed in new farmhouses and barns on the edge of town. The fighting was certain to be on foreign soil.

By early 1940 Hermann realized that the war was no "Sitzkrieg" or "phony war," as newspapers dubbed it. He abandoned hope of being transferred to Peenemünde. In fact, he feared that the rocket nest could not survive the restrictions put on it by Hitler. Because long ago der Fuehrer had turned against rockets, he now struck Peenemünde from his priority list for metals and fuels. The Luftwaffe was his magic wand of triumph.

While Hermann and the entire world waited for the last shot of battle, a bulletin that Nazi soldiers had taken Denmark and Norway came in April. Because this conquest was so fast and easy, in a month the Supreme Commander ordered an attack on Belgium, Holland, and Luxemburg. After a few weeks of fighting, these countries fell to the invader. Although the German people disapproved of this

* From *Encyclopaedia Britannica*. Chicago: Encyclopaedia Britannica, Inc., 1955, Volume 11, p. 598 B.

fighting, they dared not openly protest. The police had absolute power to suppress any resistance. Punishment was swift and brutal, even to the firing squad.

Early in June, 1940, German infantry goose-stepped into Paris and on June 25 France surrendered. Now only stubborn Britain held out to keep the war going. Hermann's thoughts returned to his experience in World War I, when England was also Germany's principal enemy. Had the Kaiser built rockets from the design Hermann had submitted, Germany might have won. Once again the same two countries faced each other, but the original rocket had grown from a picture on paper to a creature of steel and explosives. Surely the present chief of the Reich would give it a chance to win World War II.

As Hermann feared, the army reached out for his elder son. Nobody knew where Julius would be sent: possibly to England, which rumor said the Nazis intended to invade.

By August of 1940 the Battle of Britain had started. Great waves of German war planes left their bases to roar over the Channel, where they were met by British fighters, the Hurricanes and Spitfires. Each night Hermann listened to the news of that day's success. The Royal Air Force was certainly doomed. It ought to be apparent to them that Germany had the greatest air power in the world and that Hitler's Luftwaffe would yet bring victory and peace.

By September as many as 400 planes were attacking London by day and night, though German reports failed to mention that sometimes as many as fifty-six planes did not return. More planes were ordered built, then still more. The Luftwaffe program was gobbling up enormous quantities of raw materials, metals, chemicals, and fuel needed by the Peenemünde experimental station.

To save it from being closed, one general sent in "soldiers," actually craftsmen, who were listed as "being on front-line duty." The station took on a new name, the Northern Experimental Unit.

By 1941 Hitler's judgment was publicized as "infallible." The war was justified as necessary to acquire *Volksraum*, or "living space." What ordinary citizens felt about the Nazi policy they dared not utter. Almost every family had some-one in service and the Oberths worried that their daughter Ilse would be called. She was studying chemistry and the government often summoned capable girls to replace men sent into uniform.

Toward the latter part of June a bulletin was flashed which left Hermann so astonished he could hardly work at his desk. His mind would not stay on equations and draw-ings. The Reich Army had attacked the Soviets. Napoleon, a century and a half before, had invaded Russia with tragic results. Memories of his days spent facing the Cossacks be-hind the Carpathian Mountains came to Hermann's mind. Surely his son would not have to repeat that pattern. As if to soothe the father's fears, a heartening announcement was made by the High Command.

"It will all be over in six weeks!"

After two weeks the Soviets were retreating. Optimism swept the land. Russian peasants had welcomed the Nazis as heroes who were freeing them from the ruthlessness of Stalin. However, in following days, the peasants discovered they were merely being used as strong backs for hard work. Disillusioned and angry, they rallied to the Red flag, men, women, and children, and fought like demons for Mother Russia.

Six weeks passed with neither victory, armistice, nor peace. More and more boys were pulled from civilian jobs and from schools to don uniforms. Hermann looked anx-iously at his younger son, Adolf, now thirteen, tall and healthy. The military might grab him if the war were not over before winter. The Nazis, he hoped, were too smart to be trapped by the Russian snows.

In the heat of summer the Reich Army "invited" citizens to donate their skis. Men at Hermann's laboratory exchanged knowing glances: skis meant winter fighting. Reminded again of Napoleon's defeat, Hermann drew a recent drawing from his desk drawer. If only he could show the engineers at Peenemünde this improvement for the rocket.

Finally the mail brought the letter he had wanted for years. Peenemünde could use him. Come at once!

For the last time the family were together. Julius had a brief furlough before setting off for the Russian front. After a few days, luggage was packed and the group separated. Hermann boarded a train for the most secret of all German war plants, soon to work on improving the rocket he had designed so long ago. He would be among his former friends of The German Rocket Society. Once again the flight to the moon seemed near. His dream was coming true.

# *Peenemünde* [1941]

A S THE TRAIN glided through forests of tall pines, Hermann tried to remember details about Peenemünde, some of which he had received in confidence. The government had invested millions of dollars in this project, the purpose or excuse given being research on a space mirror to control world climate, a project Hermann had suggested in his first book, nearly twenty years ago. The real goal was rocketry. For this, Peenemünde had the finest electrical, structural, and hydraulic laboratories, plus the best-equipped metal and wood shops in Germany. There were a dozen test stands to hold rockets while checking their operations; also the first supersonic wind tunnel. More than seven thousand men worked on the project, over half of them prisoners of war. Yet *der Fuehrer* had stricken all this from his priority list because he disliked rockets. It did not make sense.

Hermann looked from the coach window. He was leaving civilization for a picturebook land. Everywhere he saw sand dunes, towering trees, or small lakes. The train rumbled across a drawbridge into the zone of secrecy among woods of fir and pine. It was hard to believe that in the center of this tranquil forest was a caldron of activity.

The train sped past a barracks and camp for war prisoners. It slowed down when passing a cluster of modern houses, a church with a steeple, and a school. Never had he seen so much barbed wire or so many guards. All men wore numbered badges, which he later learned, corresponded with a number on a document carried in the pocket. Badges were of different shapes and colors to identify the status of the wearer: one group was permitted only on the fringe of the establishment, another was allowed to enter certain gates, a third could penetrate various shops. Only the fourth class had permission to go into the laboratories. The heart of Peenemünde was a locked secret, and though neighboring families often heard and saw rockets launched into the sky, they knew nothing of the academic and political maneuverings within the walls.

Hermann's blood raced when he left the train and walked toward a huge gate set in a barbed-wire fence. Dr. von Braun came forward, hand outstretched, a cordial smile on his boyish face. Despite his youth, his astronautical genius had lifted him to the title of chief of technical experiments. Dr. von Braun and his former teacher made no attempt to hide their genuine delight at the reunion. Together they climbed into a large sedan.

While riding along the paved street Hermann learned that the rocket called the A-4, a shortened name for Aggregate Number Four, was facing its last chance to survive. *Der Fuehrer*, impatient with continual experimentation, demanded a long-range missile immediately. Luckily Hermann had kept informed, as much as possible, on the development of the missile. In his spare moments he had designed improvements for its parts: pumps, instruments, connections, and valves. It would not take long for him to show the Peenemünde scientists these changes. He had every reason to believe his new rocket would perform with a minimum of testing.

To Hermann's amazement he found that before he could even visit a laboratory he had to obtain clearance at the security office. A captain asked his name. Hermann told him.

"No, no," came the reply. "That's too well known. You can be . . . ahhh . . . you'll be Fritz Hann. Don't forget that name."

As the two men left the police building, they heard a roar, as if a freight train were rumbling across a wooden bridge above their heads. Hermann's eyes widened and von Braun touched his arm.

"Only an A-4 on a test stand," he shouted.

Hermann grinned. For the first time he was hearing the voice of the creature he had created on paper. He felt like a composer who, after writing a symphony, finally heard it played. He was at last to work on a real rocket, to put his vision into metal form. There would be no more frustration at seeing it only on paper or of trying to build it in a little shop with few tools.

For several hours von Braun escorted his former teacher about the grounds (Plate 8) pointing out the shops, laboratories, testing pits, and finally the Measurement House containing the flight instruments, the priceless core of the whole project. At the wind tunnel they watched through thick glass windows a model of the A-4 withstand a blast of air four times faster than sound. Farther away were other buildings among the trees, hidden from enemy reconnaissance planes. Peenemünde was carefully concealed. Even the exposed places were camouflaged. There was no danger of bombing.

At the end of the tour Hermann was taken to House No.

30, where the scientists lived. His room was modern and comfortable. A cool breeze blew in the window from the Baltic Sea, bringing with it the chatter of machines, hammers, lathes, and saws. In anticipation he thought of the dawn when he would be greeting his rocket, now much changed, matured, and almost ready for flight.

After a hearty breakfast he was shown his office, where he met the draftsman and typist assigned to him. A mound of paper work on the desk awaited his attention.

"But I am to work on rockets!" he protested.

"That is only for engineers," came the reply.

Again they had shunted him into a dead end. For days he was too ill from disappointment to sit at his desk. If only he could examine the A-4. No one was interested in the improvements he had invented. Then came an invitation to join the other scientists at a test firing and with fresh vigor he hurried to Test Stand VII.

A rocket was wheeled into the arena on a low wagon. Not until it was strung up in its metal tower did Hermann appreciate its size: forty-six feet in height with a diameter of over five feet. That was certainly a change from his sixteen-foot Model B, though the general shape had not changed. In size it looked almost like a prehistoric animal. The crew had painted it black and white to make it easier to follow against the blue of the sky. Hermann watched the technicians check every detail, valve, and both fuel tanks, one containing four tons of alcohol, the other five tons of liquid oxygen. Everything was in order. It was hard to realize that this oversized Model B would develop the energy of a million horsepower.

At a distance from the launching pad were concrete bunkers with heavy glass windows for observation. Exposed parts were painted with wavy patches to give the illusion of harmless ground shadows when seen from the sky.

Dr. von Braun signaled, and the crewmen scurried to their posts. Part of a labyrinth of cables and wires fell away. A thunderbolt of flame shot out from the nozzle. Then came an ear-splitting roar and a cyclone strong enough to topple a house. The A-4 rose toward the heavens. Then, at a height of one-half mile, all eyes upon it, the rocket exploded.

The test was another failure. How much longer would Hitler wait for them to perfect a long-range missile? Defeated again, the workers trudged back to shops and offices. Later Dr. von Braun explained that when the fragments of the rocket "fluttered" down into the sea, a bag of dye stained the water a bright green easily seen by a German pilot who guided a salvage boat to retrieve the parts for study. At this time no one knew that another A-4 would by mistake land in Sweden, giving enemy scientists a warning of coming disaster.

In the following weeks, Hermann's talent for designing rocket parts was ignored and he was assigned a routine job. All day he searched through foreign patents for what could be applied to the A-4. Discouraged, he worked automatically, the roar of motors on test stands beating against his ears. He heard the cars carrying high-echelon officers to rocket conferences. No one invited him to give his opinion. He heard trucks rumble over concrete roads and occasionally the barking of anti-aircraft guns. Often he looked up from his window to see the brownish-white trails of smoke that marked the path of Messerschmitt interceptor planes. He lived in a strange world. The heavens were filled with instruments of destruction while on the ground gardeners watered flowers. Plumbers, painters, and electricians kept the place in perfect condition, as though all were permanent and in no danger from the war.

At last Hermann maneuvered to examine an A-4. To his consternation he found that the builders had followed almost exactly his original drawings for a rocket. He had never intended his Model B as a workshop pattern. Many of the original details that he had later improved or abandoned were here in use. Unable to endure such a waste of time and money, he insisted on talking with the top man.

"This model is obsolete," he blurted. "Let me show—"

"No time," was the answer. "Hitler's war won't wait. The A-4 now goes into mass production."

Sick at heart, Hermann trudged back to his desk. It was plain the authorities had brought him to Peenemünde merely to have their fingers on him, perhaps to prevent an enemy from kidnapping him for his rocket knowledge. What good was his knowledge here when nobody would listen to him? Bitterly he thought of himself as a prisoner in a well-equipped cage. Any scientist could perform the work he had to do.

During the next weeks the fortunes of the Third Reich, as Hitler's state was called, sank lower and tension mounted at Peenemünde. Defeat hung over the Russian front. On the home front, revolt threatened. The authorities could no longer hide the enormous casualty figures. To bolster internal loyalty, the Ministry of Public Enlightenment and Culture praised a new mystery weapon, the old A-4, now christened the V-2, the V standing for *Vergeltungswaffe*, or "Retaliation Weapon." It promised to do for modern warfare what the invention of gunpowder did for the bow-and-arrow days. Only the inner circle at Peenemünde knew the V-2 had not proven reliable. Hoping to bring it up to its published reputation, the scientists forgot clocks and worked as long as they could wobble on their boots.

In desperation Dr. von Braun came to Hermann.

"Herr Professor, can you develop an Atlantic rocket to reach New York?" Nonplused by this sudden request for creative thinking, Hermann nodded and the young man hurried on. "We must get to it right away. No time to lose. Show how it will look, what will be the cost, how much fuel will be needed. Let me know as soon as possible."

Hermann lost no time getting busy on a job he liked. By December he had designed a three-stage rocket. The two lower sections were to burn first and fall into the Atlantic. Only the upper part would reach New York. The rocket nose was to carry a ton of payload, or cargo. This could mean the beginning of what he had predicted ten years back: rapid delivery from Europe to America. The two continents would be less than an hour apart. Because he disliked war, he did not like to think that the rocket could also carry tons of explosive. He preferred to dwell on the idea that eventually passengers could ride this rocket. His voice rang with enthusiasm as he phoned Dr. von Braun to come and inspect the drawings.

Before the young engineer arrived, startling news was heard on the radio. On December 7, Japan had attacked the United States by bombing Pearl Harbor in Hawaii. Hermann sank into his chair, wild ideas tumbling through his mind. Suppose the Japanese had used his new rocket? They could have bombed Pearl Harbor without the risk of sending planes. Any city across the ocean could be bombed and never know what or who hit it. There could be sudden destruction without even the warning of a declaration of war. If the rocket carried an atomic warhead, which rumors implied would soon be possible, mankind was faced with the prospect of annihilation. Hermann's deep integrity caused him to think of the moral responsibility for the rocket he had just designed. His hand reached for the drawing. He would tear it up. Yet such an act would be disobedient to his command, a deadly crime during war. Dare he risk that? He heard boots approaching his door. Only one man walked with such optimism, as though his thoughts were on the way to Venus and Mars. Dr. von Braun entered the room to see the design of the world's largest rocket.

**CHAPTER 14** ♜ "To land, sea and air may now be added infinite empty space as an area of future intercontinental traffic, thereby acquiring political importance."

WALTER DORNBERGER

# The Birth of Space Travel [1942]

ALTHOUGH DR. VON BRAUN was pleased with Hermann's design, he dared not order it into production until the V-2's had been perfected. His men believed they were erasing the last flaws. By June they planned a full-scale testing which all felt would put Peenemünde back on Hitler's priority list.

On the day of the firing, men gathered on the roofs and in the windows from which they could view Test Stand VII. Above the noise of machinery the loudspeaker blared.

"X minus three!"

Hermann's heart was hammering so loudly he scarcely heard the "X minus two." One minute was left. Almost at once green smoke was visible.

"Ignition!"

Steel cables dropped. Thunder began. The V-2 started

up. Hermann was following the flight with strong binoculars when, at an altitude of about five and one-half miles, the nose cone containing the payload came loose. Unable to balance without this load, the giant rocket broke into pieces.

Dr. Dornberger (Plate 9) was the first to speak, despair and determination in his tone. They must try again and then again.

In silence the men returned to their jobs and Hermann to his desk. He was not happy. While he was living in comfort, Tilly's letters told of the hardships others were enduring. When shoes became scarce the people were told that it was healthier to go barefoot, yet the High Command all wore boots. To compensate for the scarcity of cigars and cigarettes, civilians were warned that tobacco was harmful. Restrictions were many: no one must listen to British or Moscow broadcasts; if foreign planes dropped leaflets they must be gathered unread and handed to the police. Wild rumors swept the land. Germany had a bomb to destroy twenty square miles with each shell and thus bring the British king to his knees. By a fabulous trick, England would suddenly be frozen with artificial ice. London was to be incinerated by rays from a space mirror. To scatter the fear of defeat on the Russian front Dr. Goebbels reminded the people of Frederick the Great, whose courage had saved "Germanic substance." "But," civilians countered, "what is that?"

Hermann worried about the safety of his family. A few scientists had been permitted to move their families to Peenemünde, but he was not convinced that the rocket center could escape bombing. Of course no place was completely safe. From cities came reports of traitorous bombings with "Molotov cocktails," homemade grenades fashioned from empty bottles filled with gasoline and explosives.

They were tossed at military persons and equipment. As resistance to the Government soared, each morning found new scribbling on walls and fences: "Down with Hitler!" Revolt could break out any hour.

The men at the rocket nest tried to hurry their work on the V-2 and by August were ready for another test. Hopes rose only to be dashed into failure. Again the men bent over desks and workbenches. Another anxiety added to their fear that Hitler would not wait: the V-2 had competition for his favor. The air force had brought out a winged rocket known officially as the FI-103, but generally called the V-1. Later, England was to nickname them "Buzz Bombs."

The V-1 was not a true rocket, because it drew its oxygen from the air; a real rocket is not dependent on the atmosphere. It looked like a small plane with a fusilage about twenty-five feet in length and a wing spread of approximately eighteen feet. It had the disadvantage of flying comparatively slowly (360 miles per hour), which made it a target for anti-aircraft and plane gunners. Yet it also had advantages which *der Fuehrer* liked. A V-1 cost only one-tenth the price of a V-2 and was simple to handle and transport. In addition, the V-1 did not require special fuel. This was a big item in its favor, since the Allies were blasting German chemical sources.

Then Hermann's group received another blow. When it was pointed out to the High Command that the V-1 could replace planes and thus save pilots from British bullets, a hundred launching sites for the rocket were ordered. Men of the V-2 were in despair. The launching ramps were long strips of cement, which would consume an enormous amount of that material needed at Peenemünde. Their engineers had hoped to get enough to build a huge underground workshop for the V-2, a sort of cavern protected by a concrete roof over twenty feet thick. Because of the bombed roads cement was difficult to obtain. Much of it had been sent to build what Hitler called his "Atlantic Wall" to defend Fortress Europe. In reality, this was not a wall but a network of obstacles intended to protect the beaches against Allied invasion. The system included concrete teeth set under water to rip the hulls of boats, buried mines, pillbox forts, and machine-gun nests, all connected by trenches and tangles of barbed wire.

Hermann shared the desperation of those working on the V-2, but at last the rocket was ready for another test. If this failed, Peenemünde was finished. October 3rd was set for the trial.

Dawn brought a cloudless sky. Workmen gathered on the flat roofs. Holding his binoculars, Hermann had the feeling of a father about to witness the graduation of a child. He felt that the rocket was his, since it was so obviously built after his pattern. At the scheduled time, gates nearly a hundred feet tall opened and the V-2 was rolled from the hall where it had been assembled. Hydraulic machinery set it on a launching pad as if it were a toy. The servicing scaffold moved like a house on wheels, the workers on it resembling dwarfs. The whole affair seemed like a dream. Once again the loudspeaker began the countdown. Peenemünde minutes seemed longer than any in the world. Hermann kept his eyes on a stopwatch. Fifty seconds left, thirty, ten. Now!

"Ignition!" blared the intercommunication system.

An engineer moved a switch. Clouds and sparks shot from the throat of the thirteen-ton monster. A second switch was pulled. Fire and thunder belched out. Smoke and dust blasted across the area and struck the protective bunkers. A final switch was thrown. At a signal, a cable dropped. Over fifty thousand pounds of thrust boosted the rocket. At first slowly then with increasing speed it moved straight upward as if gliding on rails (Plate 10).

Hermann pressed his eyes to his glasses. Against the azure sky the black-and-white markings showed that the giant was not spinning. Its gyroscope was operating perfectly. A shrill sound drifted back to the earth. If only Tilly could see this! thought Hermann. She had always believed his rocket would fly. Gradually he became aware that the launching control was counting over the loudspeaker: ten, twenty.

Hermann's pulse nearly stopped. This time there was no explosion and no accident. Hats were thrown from the rooftops into the air, accompanied by shouts and laughter. In an instant men were shaking hands and wiping tears of joy from their eyes.

That evening the scientists held a celebration of the triumph of their V-2. Speeches were made to point up the importance of the day's test. The rocket had definitely proven that: (1) It was possible to fly with automatic guidance. (2) The V-2 could be controlled at the fantastic speed of 3,600 miles per hour. (3) Rocket propulsion would operate in airless space.

One man stressed the military significance. The V-2 rocket was destined to revolutionize warfare. The era of big cannons was ended. Future weapons would be rockets. The old altitude record for the famous Paris Gun had been broken at last. That huge gun had been the terror of World War I because it lobbed shells onto the French capital from a forest seventy-six miles away. Those shells had reached the then-fabulous height of twenty-five miles. Today's V-2 had soared sixty miles above the earth and traveled 120 miles.

Another speaker claimed that the record of the V-2

would be as trivial to future space travel as the flight of the Wright Brothers compared with trans-ocean airplanes. Orville Wright flew at a speed of thirty miles an hour. In 1903 very few could foresee flying around the world. Yet that first flight of fifty-nine seconds had put mankind into the air. The demonstration of October 3, 1942, would catapult man into outer space.

Major Dornberger closed the evening. After praising his faithful laboratory and work crews he concluded:

"We have invaded space with our rocket and for the first time—mark this well—have used space as a bridge between two points on the earth; we have proved rocket propulsion practicable for space travel. . . . Development of possibilities we cannot yet envisage will be a peacetime task. Then the first thing will be to find a safe means of landing after the journey through space. . . ." *

The room shook with applause. Hermann joined the others in talk of bigger rockets and of trips to planets. All felt certain that when the report of that day's success reached the High Command, the treasury would send funds for raw materials and fuel.

Leaving the building, Hermann personally congratulated the Major.

"But, Professor," came the astonished reply, "the congratulation goes to you for showing us the way."

Hermann could not believe his ears. He could find no words except a mumbled thanks. It was unbelievable that he was receiving credit for the rocket and still was not permitted to work on it. He walked to his room, never suspecting that across the English Channel a clock was already ticking the destruction of Peenemünde.

* From V-2, by Walter Dornberger. New York: Viking Press, 1958, p. 17.

**CHAPTER 15** ♜ "It seemed likely that, if the German had succeeded in perfecting and using these new weapons six months earlier than he did, our invasion of Europe would have proved exceedingly difficult, perhaps impossible."

DWIGHT D. EISENHOWER

# The Bombing of Peenemünde [1943]

FTER THE REPORT of the triumphal firing of the V-2 had been dispatched to Berlin, all Peenemünde breathed with fresh hope. Any day the needed steel and fuel would arrive. But nothing came, not even extra workers to replace those drafted to carry guns. Since it was customary for researchers to have a special project and since Hermann could do little more on the V-2, he began to cast about for something vitally needed. It was becoming more difficult to keep his thoughts from conditions at home. Tilly's letters distressed him. While he had heat to keep warm, civilian houses were cold. To keep from freezing Tilly wore several sweaters. Everything was rationed, even such essentials as potatoes and bread. Working men and women were often paid in food coupons instead of money. Wives hoarded bottles in hope of finding something to preserve in them. Every night more families were bombed out of their homes and had to move in with friends or possibly with strangers.

No one dared complain lest they be shipped to a labor camp. The only sign of relief was the promised "wonder weapon" that was to end the war swiftly and triumphantly.

In February a shocking bulletin came from the Russian front. Winter had allied herself with the Soviets. A German general and two hundred thousand boys had surrendered. Hermann had special reason for alarm. Perhaps his son was among them. He heard that Russia sent prisoners to camps in frozen Siberia.

Although the Professor went daily to his desk, there was no incentive to work. The shops stood idle for lack of materials, and scarcity of fuel halted activity on the testing stands. Repeatedly Colonel Dornberger went to the High Command with his list of needs, returning each time only with vague promises. Then in March *der Fuehrer* dreamed that "No V-2 would ever reach England." The dream to him was the same as fact.

Once again Colonel Dornberger and Dr. von Braun prepared to argue with their Chief. Hermann and other scientists watched the two men set off for Berlin. They took with them a film of the successful flight and a wooden model of the V-2. Not only the future of Peenemünde, but perhaps that of rocketry, depended on this trip.

It seemed a long wait until the two men returned, weary yet encouraged. Hitler had promised top priority. Instead of rejoicing, many of the scientists thought it was already too late to save the Reich. Hermann offered no opinion. He was only a cog in the giant army wheel.

By June a new order came. Put the V-2 into immediate mass production! Everyone at Peenemünde knew the rocket was not ready for an assembly line. Its performance was not reliable and more testing was necessary. But Hitler was impatient and demanded that thirty thousand rockets be ready for an all-out attack by October. This was impossible for several reasons: there was a shortage of manpower and fuels; certain parts were scarce because roads had been bombed and no company dared guarantee a shipment. In addition, factories producing necessary chemicals had been blasted out of business so chemists had to hunt for substitutes.

When Dornberger, now a general, agreed to try to turn out thirty rockets a day, nine hundred a month, *der Fuehrer* waved his magic wand over Peenemünde. Buses carried in workers, loaded trucks brought supplies, and soon the machinery was humming. Hermann too caught the feeling of optimism. Secure and busy, he did not suspect that the V-2 had already sown the seed of its own destruction. A vapor trail against the blue sky had been spied by Swedes and Frenchmen, who relayed this news to the British Secret Service.

Ordinarily, no one at Peenemünde attached any dire meaning to the whir of Royal Air Force planes overhead. Reconnaissance pilots could see almost nothing because of the dense woods and the camouflage. As an extra precaution the authorities regularly tested the air-raid warning system. Every man knew his battle station or his shelter. Inspectors checked at each twilight to make sure the blackout was thorough. The inhabitants of the rocket center had good reason to feel safe when they retired on the night of August 17th.

Hermann went early to his room. A peaceful breeze fluttered the curtains at his window. While he was writing to Tilly, the sirens wailed an "early alarm." He was used to that. The sound merely meant that once again British bombers were massing over the Baltic. As usual, the report on the radio presumed that Berlin was their target, so the Professor went to bed.

Scarcely had he gone to sleep when he was awakened by sirens giving the signal for action. He arose as he had been trained, grabbed the suitcase kept packed with his most valuable documents, gave a farewell look at the books he could not take with him, and padded out of the building. Overhead a full moon was shining. Noting the odd black angles cast by the camouflaged roofs, he thought it was unlikely that these could be detected from the height of planes.

Standing in front of the shelter bunker to which he had been assigned he waited for an "all-clear" signal. It was a gentle summer night with no hint of disaster. A fog had drifted in from the sea as if to slumber on the land. The scientists stood around in the eerie light, speaking of the possibility of reaching the moon, or perhaps Mars. Not daring to return to bed until the all-clear signal, they lingered wearily. Conversation died. The night was hushed except for the ever-present whir of machinery.

About two in the morning Hermann thought he heard a different sound. Was it possible the bombers had veered from the capital? Even before he felt sure, the advance herald, a "Christmas tree" flare, appeared in the air. Dropped from a plane, it turned night into day at ground level, floating like a giant Yule tree with candles and harmless baubles. Gradually the telltale odor seeped through the cottony swirls of fog. There was no doubt now. Peenemünde had been marked for attack. With other scientists, Hermann entered the shelter to which he had been assigned.

Waves of four-motored bombers roared overhead. They crisscrossed like a drill team, laying down what was called a bomb carpet. Anti-aircraft went into action. Enormous searchlights raked the sky to pinpoint the targets. Still the bombers came, six hundred strong, to drop three million pounds of explosives plus countless stick incendiaries that burst and splattered tongues of flame. Soon the fog turned red from burning buildings and trees. The air quivered from the thunderous impact of heavy bombs, the drone of motors, the crack of anti-aircraft, the tinkle of falling glass, and the snap of fire.

When the bunkers shuddered as if about to collapse, it was apparent to the men that this was no routine bombing. Everything might be lost. Calling to those near him, Hermann led a brigade from the shelter. All night he darted among falling debris, trying to save documents and vital designs. Firemen were fighting flames. A canteen service managed to bring in coffee and soup. The air churned with smoke and flying cinders from explosions.

Dawn revealed a bizarre sight: iron girders clawing over smoldering ruins, gaunt chimneys rising above fallen walls and roads blocked with rubble. Where laboratories had stood only a few hours ago, now empty craters gaped (Plate 11). Later it was learned that under the ruins lay over seven hundred bodies, including many top scientists.

General Dornberger inspected the havoc. There was no possibility of men returning to their usual tasks. The place must be either rebuilt at once or abandoned. Hermann awaited the decision. Finally it came: Peenemünde could not be given up; the government had spent too much money there not to try to salvage it. To trick the Royal Air Force into thinking destruction was complete, the men shoveled the debris into conspicuous piles. A few buildings were repaired enough for workers to return to desks and shops.

The war would not wait. The High Command still wanted thirty V-2's a day.

Hermann read his own anxiety in the faces around him. Would the "frozen lightning," the vapor trails from test firing, again betray activity at Peenemünde? He wondered if the enemy reconnaissance planes overhead were taking pictures. He watched the roads being cleared for the supply trucks. If only he could walk down one of those roads and out the gate. But he had already learned that a man working for the German Army did not put on his hat and leave.

Several weeks later he was awarded the Cross of Merit with the Swords for his efforts in saving Peenemünde. He would have preferred discharge papers freeing him to return to Tilly and his own personal space research.

By December it was apparent from repeated bombings that the Allies were clearing the coast for invasion of Europe. Despite Hitler's demands, the V-2 rockets could not be delivered since it was impossible to get the separate parts with which to put them together. All young men of gun-carrying age had again been called into the army and there was a shortage of workers. To fill the gaps, prisoners were brought in to work under the supervision of trusted Nazis, but the new men dallied at their jobs, their thoughts on escape. It was no secret that the guards were open to bribery.

At last the Supreme Headquarters announced that Peenemünde must provide anti-aircraft rockets for defense. One already in use was the *Wasserfall* or "Waterfall," which looked like a half-size V-2 with four stubby wings. It stood about twenty-five feet tall and was launched like the V-2. Flying at supersonic speed, and equipped with a mechanical brain, it was expected to climb to the height of enemy bombers, then charge them head-on or chase them away. But only one rocket in four behaved as expected. The design needed improving. This meant test firing, and already enemy spies were alerted to watch for vapor trails. Though apprehensive, the men were prepared to go to any lengths to save the Third Reich.

Each day brought more tragic dispatches. German spies reported that General Dwight D. Eisenhower had set up headquarters in England. Allied planes began around-the-clock bombing, the United States during the day, the Royal Air Force at night. There was no sleep in all Germany. Civilian morale was cracking. At Peenemünde, each breakfast meant more empty place at the tables.

With the coming of snow a broadcast announced that the Soviets, undaunted by hardships, were slogging forward through a blizzard. Whispers said that a spearhead was aiming for Peenemünde. The German soldiers were almost helpless on frozen ground. The scientists stood in their warm lounge discussing means for defending themselves behind wire barricades; surely there would be no street fighting. Over and above personal safety, they were concerned about the top-secret drawings. These must not fall into Russian hands, but no one wanted to destroy them. Perhaps they could be carted away to a secret cave. Not one man dared voice the question in all minds: was Hitler's Thousand-Year-Reich approaching its twilight?

In a final effort to save Deutschland, General Dornberger turned to the defensive rocket. Years before, Professor Oberth had told the military about an anti-aircraft missile he had invented to run on a cheap solid fuel made of coal, water, and air. Those raw materials were about all that was available, and even coal was scarce. But possibly he could perfect his missile in a short time.

However, Peenemünde was not equipped for research on solid propellants. All equipment was for liquid-fuel experiments. So the General combed Germany for a place which would be safe from bombing and also provide facilities for Hermann's work. The Wittenberg district filled both requirements. It had been the home of Martin Luther, the great German reformer who had challenged the authority of the Pope in the sixteenth century. The town, its roots deep in sacred history, had an atmosphere of serenity, and it was expected that enemy bombers would spare its shrines. Also, there was a famous high-explosives factory where the Professor could develop his rocket.

Hermann left the rocket center with mixed emotions. It seemed that Peenemünde was pushing him out after taking all it could get from him. His new assignment appeared almost impossible. In a short time they expected him to build a guided anti-aircraft rocket capable of bringing down enemy bombers over the Baltic before they reached the homeland. It was a large order, but he would do all he could to save the Reich.

# CHAPTER 16 ♜ "Wisdom is better than weapons of war; but one sinner destroyeth much good."

ECCLESIASTES 8:18

# Germany's Death Struggle [1944]

**H**ERMANN DID NOT REGRET leaving the sea breezes of Peenemünde for a safer inland town. Riding on the train past gaunt shells of houses, he had the comforting reminder that his family was safe. They had moved to a house in Feucht, near Nürnberg, which his father had sent money to buy. The place was known as the "little castle," because it had space around it for a garden. Most houses were built wall to wall. Tilly and young Adolf could raise vegetables and assure themselves of a food supply.

Arriving in Reinsdorf, in central Germany, he was assigned a sleeping room by the Housing Office. Then he reported to the Westfälisch-Anhaltische Springstoff A.G. (Westphalian-Anhaltian Explosives Company), or

WASAG, where he was to work in an office shared by three other men. The company was an old firm famous for making high explosives.

The month of February moved on and off the calendar without a bombardment of England. Neither the V-1's nor the V-2's were ready for a mass attack. The factory in which the V-2's were assembled was in the caves near Nordhausen, from where the rockets were hauled back to Peenemünde for testing. However, though Nordhausen turned out about six hundred rockets a month, there was no fuel to test them. In March the ominous rumor came from Peenemünde that Dr. von Braun had been arrested and sentenced to death for obstructing the war effort with his nonsense about space travel. Only Dornberger's words had saved him: "No von Braun, no V-2!"

Ignoring the clock, Hermann worked at laboratory and desk. Sleep was nearly impossible under the nightly roar of British Lancaster bombers, each carrying eight tons of "blockbusters" to some unlucky German city. These bombs were so named because one could shatter a city block. By day it was hard to concentrate against the sound of American Flying Fortresses heading for a railroad center or fuel dump. Adding to their noise was that of the escorting long-range fighters.

By the time Hermann had almost perfected a rocket operating on ammonium nitrate, that chemical was no longer available. His large solid-fuel missile could not be built unless he found a substitute. It seemed like a futile treadmill. Perhaps the aim of the Casablanca Conference was coming true. At this meeting, Roosevelt and Churchill had reviewed the war and set their goal, the "destruction and dislocation of the German military, industrial and economic system and the undermining of the morale of the

German people to the point where their capacity for armed resistance was fatally weakened." *

Every day Hermann faithfully went to his office and tried to work but since no trucks brought supplies, there was almost nothing to use except his pencils. A radio was kept on in hope of good news, but unlike his fellow workers who watched for a barrage of the mystery weapons to knock England from the war, Hermann could not draw courage from the promises of the High Command. He had learned the truth at Peenemünde: there was no fuel to get the rockets off the ground.

Shortly after midnight of June 5th he was awakened by unusual excitement in the streets. An unbelievable message had come in from France: "Allied paratroops landing in Normandy!" All Germany awaited a bulletin from military headquarters. Then it came. This was no major attack on Fortress Europe. The weather was not right, and the rising tide would make it impossible for the invaders to clear landing channels among the obstacles on the beaches. Allied paratroopers were merely sneaking in more supplies to the French Underground. There was no cause for alarm: they would be hunted down and destroyed as in the past.

Not until later did Hermann learn that twelve thousand Americans had dropped from carrier planes, and later four thousand from noiseless gliders. With their faces blackened, the men could not be seen in the shadows of bush and swamp. Before the defenders realized what was happening the invaders from the sky had captured the causeways, roads built through the swamp from the shore inland. No one suspected that the Allied soldiers had

* From the *Encyclopaedia Britannica*. Chicago: Encyclopaedia Britannica, Inc., 1955, Vol. 1, p. 460.

exact maps showing every tree and bridge, or that this invasion had been carefully rehearsed.

By dawn the High Command had more than paratroops to worry them. The Channel was alive with ships. Never in all history had there been such a concentration of military might. German officers watched in stupefaction while the Allies actually began building an artificial harbor of concrete sections and old boats. Over the gutted land the civilians clustered around radios, their only solace in a toppling world. But the war dispatches only bewildered them further. It could not be true, the broadcast said, that the big guns of Allied warships were blasting the Atlantic Wall or that Allied soldiers were pouring out of four thousand transport ships to wade ashore. Germany's fleet of U-boats made this impossible. The broadcast neglected to mention that 640 German submarines had been sunk.

With the coming of daylight the workers began entering WASAG. Some were stunned, others flung aside their fear of the Gestapo and voiced bitter words. The most fanatical Nazi loyalty was faltering. Hermann heard one question that brought him up with a jolt. Would they be tried as war criminals for their work on war explosives? Hermann thought of his home in Feucht. Tilly and young Adolf were safe. But where could *he* find safety?

The men settled at their desks and benches. Hermann lifted his pencil but he could not concentrate on the figures before him. From the next room came the excited voice of a radio announcer. Millions of foreign soldiers were wading ashore. Millions of trucks were coming onto the beaches. Millions? It was incredible to think that the island of Britain could have hidden so many men and vehicles, plus the necessary carloads of food, ammunition, and fuel! Why had German reconnaissance planes not seen them? Nothing made sense. Leaving his chair, he went to join his fellow workers. There was a feeling of security in being together.

During the day more discouraging flashes came over the air. The French Underground had blown up railroad tracks and locomotives, so German reinforcements could not be rushed to the Normandy Beach. Due to the continued lack of fuel, Luftwaffe planes could not rise to give battle. Almost the only aircraft in the sky were painted with candy stripes, marking them as belonging to the Allies.

Finally heartening news arrived. *Der Fuehrer,* informed of the invasion as he was about to dine with distinguished guests, had smiled and announced that there was no need for panic. His Atlantic Wall would endure longer than the Great Wall of China. The rising tide would drown any invaders trying to wade in with guns and equipment, and those few reaching the sandy shore would trip off his land mines. These were plastic saucers filled with explosives and buried in the sand to be detonated by the pressure of a foot. In addition, there were the guns in his pillbox forts. No allied umbrella of planes could save their men from the most senseless slaughter in all history.

By the end of the week part of this prophecy had come true. The invasion had bogged down. Then Germans heard good news over their radios. The long-awaited V-1's developed at Peenemünde by the Luftwaffe were at last raining destruction on England. When their supply bases were wiped out the Allies would have to surrender. But the High Command did not mention that the V-1 rocket was inaccurate. Before launching, its rudder was roughly set for direction and drift and it was kept on course by an automatic pilot. Moreover, it gave warning of its approach, because it created a great noise as it zoomed across the sky. The German people did not learn that of the approximate eight thousand V-1's fired, less than a third ever reached London. Many were shot down, and others were trapped in wires and chains dangling from a canopy of balloons over the city.

Day after day Hermann reported for work at WASAG. The town had not been bombed, perhaps because the Russians were heading toward it and the Allies preferred to spend their attacks on factories. Since work was impossible without supplies, the men turned to conversation about the mystery weapon soon to end the war. They did not know that a V-2 giant had already arrived in London packed in a box. Fired from Peenemünde, it had fallen in Sweden, where the fragments were gathered and flown to England. After shocked British scientists had pieced together the scraps, Churchill reported the facts to his people. They must gird themselves for the worst. The nozzle of this coming monster was large enough for a man to crawl through and sit in its burning-chamber. There was positively no defense against it, since by calculation, it would move too fast to be shot down or even seen. England's crucial hour had come: The Empire hung in the balance.

On September 6 the first two V-2 rockets left their pads for Paris, which had been taken by the Allies a month before: one hit, one fell short. Two days later the first of 3,000 V-2's was launched toward London. During daylight, V-2 motors were given a hot test and sent to a launching site at the rate of one almost every fifteen minutes. Victory or defeat for the Reich hung on the rocket's vapory trail.

All summer Hermann worked on equations and formulas and in his spare moments listened to broadcasts. Hoping to lift his thoughts from depressing war bulletins, he began drawing a moon car. Little by little a definite design took shape in his mind. For exercise he walked to the Lutheran shrines. In the town, civilians were trying to ignore their shabby clothing and empty stores. The brightest moment of any day was the arrival of a letter from home.

Then came terrible news. His daughter Ilse, who had taken a position as a chemist to release a man to fight, had been killed in an explosion. Moreover, their son Julius was missing. Both were heroes without citations. Fortunately, Adolf was much too young to be summoned for service. The war might be over by the time he reached military age.

The fortunes of the Reich worsened. The army reached for both older and younger males, and Adolf, only fourteen, was called. Buttoning on a uniform, he took his place at an anti-aircraft unit. When enemy planes arrived his boyish hands helped fire the flak.

To the consternation of Germany the use of their mighty V-2 rockets did not slacken the invasion. Behind the first million Allied invaders came thousands more, bringing gasoline, rubber tires, ammunition, and food, all of which were scarce in the Reich. Between ground battles and aerial bombing, roads were gutted and communications choked off. From a man escaping from Transylvania, Hermann heard that the Russians had captured Rumania and that the Soviet flag now flew over Schaessburg. Though Dr. Julius Oberth had survived, the fate of other relatives was not as good. A favorite cousin had been carried off with others to work in Soviet mines or factories. Hermann remembered that Moscow wanted rocket experts. What would be his fate if he were captured by the Russians or by the Allies? He must be ready to make a decision.

# CHAPTER 17 ♖

"Of all the tyrannies on human kind,
The worst is that which persecutes the mind."

JOHN DRYDEN

# A Captive and a Wanderer [1945-1950]

Through the Christmas season Hermann wondered what his family was doing. Would Tilly decorate the usual tree? Perhaps Adolf was home on furlough. What kind of festivity would his father have under the Russian flag? Not for an hour of day or night was Hermann allowed to forget that armies were hammering Germany on two fronts. From information reaching WASAG it appeared that the death rattle of the Third Reich was beginning. Hermann watched every Nazi policeman with apprehension, recalling the rumor at Peenemünde that S.S. Troops had secret orders to liquidate scientists to prevent them from falling into Allied camps. No one knew if this was fact or fiction. Dr. von Braun believed the government might use space engineers as hostages to dicker for easier terms in the event of defeat.

Hermann kept his few valuable possessions in a suitcase. For safety he hid the scientific autobiography he had written in a cave. Its thirteen hundred pages were too heavy to carry. He was ready to flee at a moment's notice, but where could he escape both the enemy and freezing storms? He dared not go to his father in Schaessburg or to Tilly in Feucht, since home was the first place the Allies would look for him. Furthermore, there was no prospect of renting a room in an obscure town since every building was registered and every room assigned by some Housing Office.

In January, desperation seized the top-echelon officers. Hitler called for "every sacrifice" and "utmost fanaticism." Conflicting orders reached WASAG as to what to do with the partially finished anti-aircraft rockets. Reports came that Peenemünde was to be abandoned and its work transferred to caves near Nordhausen. Already the thunder of Russian cannon could be heard at the V-2 testing stands and Dr. von Braun did not think the Cossacks were far behind. To discuss the possibility of surrender, he called a secret meeting of his scientists. Lest they be caught by the Gestapo in what would be considered treason they gathered in a farmhouse. Von Braun came directly to the point.

"Germany has lost the war. But let us not forget that it was our team that first succeeded in reaching outer space. . . . Each of the conquering powers will want our knowledge. The question we must answer is: To what country shall we entrust our heritage?" *

Without one negative vote the men agreed to surrender to the American Army.

When it was later determined that Peenemünde could not be saved, the S.S. Troops were ordered to escort all documents to a secret place for future use. Tons of material

* From *Reaching for the Stars*, by Erik Bergaust. Garden City, L.I.: Doubleday & Company, Inc., 1960, p. 106.

and thousands of men began to move, despite the chaos of roads and rails. By day and night, over almost every available highway, the rumble of motor convoys could be heard. In order to see in the darkness yet not attract enemy bombers, some had been equipped with infrared-light devices.

March was a fateful month. The first shock was the fall of Peenemünde to the Russian Army. Hoping to counterbalance this blow, the German radio boasted that already 9,300 V-1 rockets had been fired on London. When this produced no burst of patriotism, the Propaganda Ministry reported that since over one thousand of the giant V-2's had been lobbed onto England, British surrender might come with the next ton of explosives. The announcer did not mention that there would be no "next" rocket. The last one had roared from its launching pad.

By this time the population of Germany was too worried to care about offensive war. Their own towns were ablaze. Along the pitted roads frantic families moved, searching for places to hide from the fire, din, stench of death, and bitter cold.

It was not long before the remaining loyal Nazis suffered another blow. Allied soldiers had entered the Nordhausen caves (Plate 12). Under what Americans called Operation Paper Clip they began scooping up uncompleted rockets and boxing them to ship to the United States. They found enough V-2's to fill three hundred boxcars.

Hermann and the men at WASAG decided to face the blunt facts. The end of the Third Reich was near. Even the loyal Minister of German Munitions, Albert Speer, admitted, "German economy is heading for inevitable collapse within four to eight weeks." * Hermann surveyed his

---

* From the *Encyclopaedia Britannica*. Chicago: Encyclopaedia Britannica, Inc., Vol. I, p. 476.

future. Since both Russians and Americans now had V-2 parts, they would be hunting for scientists to show them how to put the rockets together. If captured, he would become a prisoner-of-war, and no doubt would be shipped to either Russia or the United States. In either case, he would be separated from his family. He must save himself.

The month of May opened with the broadcast of Hitler's death. Confusion gripped the Reich. The end had come.

With two other men from WASAG, Hermann left Reinsdorf. They trudged through Bavaria, occasionally managing to ride. Railroad stations had been gutted by bombs. Ducks paddled in spring ponds formed by shell holes. At shipping centers crooked rails were twisted among the skeletons of burned coaches. All street signs had vanished. Few houses had windows. Some had a few sheep tethered on front lawns. In many towns the Labor Office gave refugees the job of clearing away rubble, paying them in butter, bacon, or stove wood. Merchants did not want new customers, since they had little to sell. Every street echoed with the creak of carts. Children tugged little red wagons piled with kindling salvaged from ruins; women pulled carts containing potatoes. Bigger vehicles formerly drawn by horses were hauled by men.

It seemed as if everyone were either fleeing or trying to reach home. Some citizens had passes to travel from zone to zone; others sneaked over by night. Only those with passes could get food cards at a city hall and be assigned to a billet. If Hermann was lucky, at twilight, he had a straw mattress, at rare times a feather bed. At night owls hooted in the empty shells of houses. By dawn he was again on the road. If he was lucky at noon, he ate bread with a paper-twist of salt. Sometimes there was the luxury of beets, red cabbage, or even potato dumplings with brown gravy.

On to Bavaria went the three men from WASAG. They

saw children treasure-hunting in bombed ruins and parents painting over the black shadows put on doors by the Gestapo, lifesize figures in huge black hats holding a warning finger to the lips. Swastikas were being jerked down from public buildings with a spirit of sadness and relief. Often the white flags of surrender still fluttered from upper windows. Broken rifles lay abandoned by soldiers who had surrendered. In town squares guns had been put into piles when their owners disappeared.

It was with a confusion of emotion that Hermann finally accepted capture. The American Army took him at Regensburg in Bavaria, the town from which early Christianity had spread to Germany. The center for the manufacture of Messerschmitt fighter planes, it had been a special target for the Allies.

Hour after hour he was quizzed about his knowledge of rockets. After a few days he was shipped to a chateau at Le Chesnay outside Versailles, which was guarded by sentinels day and night. Though all prisoners there had physical comforts, they were forbidden to talk to each other. Again and again they were called for interrogation and after each session Hermann hoped to be discharged. Finally he was instructed to prepare for travel and was taken by car to Kronberg in the Taunus Mountains near the Rhine River.

Here he was quartered in an elegant mansion said to have been a vacation spot of Hermann Goering, the head of the Luftwaffe. Again he was interrogated until his patience wore thin. Since simple replies did not win his release, he decided to try another tactic. At the next questioning he pretended to have trouble remembering. "I'm sorry, sir," he would stammer, "I guess I was not sufficiently interested in that detail to remember it."

How well his trick worked was recorded by Dr. Fritz Zwicky, one of the team of American scientists who examined German prisoners. While he was obviously annoyed at Hermann's sudden lack of memory, he had to admit that the Professor was the first man to promote the idea of rocketry. After writing a brief biography of the prisoner, Dr. Zwicky continued:

> Oberth belongs to the class of unfortunate amateur-type individuals who pick up an idea early, who advocate the idea, and who find no response. Later, when the idea is taken up and developed by competent professionals, there remains nothing for the original advocate but to reminisce on the past. . . . One of his pupils was Freiherr Wernher von Braun, later director at Peenemünde. . . .*

Hermann's joy on being released was marred by the order to report to Allied Headquarters every other day, which meant he could not leave Germany. Tilly wept for joy when he appeared at the door of their "little castle." She had lived in fear that he would be sent to a far country with other rocket engineers.

But life at home was not easy. There was scarcely space for him in his own house. The authorities had billeted so many refugees there that he and Tilly had to be content with two small rooms. Adolf was studying chemistry at Regensburg. While the tenants quarreled, Hermann settled at a little bedside table to start writing his next book.

Feeling sure that his education and experience would benefit him, he went to apply for a steady position as a teacher. Dozens of names were ahead of his. Each day he became less particular about what type of work he obtained. Although he was willing to accept any job that paid, he found no openings. Hermann wondered if he had not blundered in leaving the Americans. Perhaps he should have

---

* From *Report on Certain Phases of War Research in Germany*, by Fritz Zwicky. Headquarters Air Materiel Command, January, 1947.

admitted that the giant rockets had grown from his original
ideas and even had the shape of his old Model B. But since
his own countrymen gave him no credit, it would have been
hard to convince the United States that the V-2 had details
shown in his earlier drawings and writings, such as the
arrangement of fuel tanks, combination of propellants, and
fins in the exhaust stream to stabilize the rocket's flight.
Now it was too late. The United States had sent more than
120 German scientists to work in their laboratories. Most of
his friends from Peenemünde were in the group supervised
by his former pupil, von Braun, whose success made Hermann question again his wisdom in refusing to cooperate
with the Americans. Would fate always let him only peer
into his Promised Land of rocketry, never to enter?

The currency reform of 1948 left German pockets empty.
The Reichsmark was converted into new Deutsche marks at
the rate of ten to one. Most of the bank savings were held
and a large per cent later canceled. Citizens were glad to
work merely for food, without demanding money.

Failing to find a position in Feucht, Hermann wrote to
foreign countries. When an offer came from Switzerland he
accepted it. This raised a new question: how could he cross
the border without the proper papers? He determined to
try. With another man he hiked to the boundary and
stayed at a local inn. The landlady was sympathetic to men
trying to get work and support their families. Since tourists
were identified by the rucksacks, or packs, on their backs,
the men decided to masquerade as Swiss natives who were
at the border to visit relatives. Hermann put on all the
clothing he could struggle into and gave the balance to his
landlady. In return she declared him a mountain guide.
Using this classification and his pseudonym, Fritz Hann,
he found that the gates swung open to admit him to Switzerland.

The promised work was not as steady as he had expected. He gave technical advice and wrote for magazines, but he had to be cautious because foreigners were not permitted to earn money belonging to local labor. During this time he contacted other places that might furnish steady employment.

In 1950 a letter came from the Italian Government. Their navy had good reason to be interested in the ammonium-nitrate rocket he had been "secretly" developing at the WASAG. During the war, the Italian submarine embankment, two miles long, had been blasted by aerial bombs. Since then, the war chemists had tried in vain to perfect his anti-aircraft missile. Would he come to help them? His reply was simple: indeed he would!

Again he faced the problem of crossing a national boundary without proper papers. Moreover, Italy had a law against employing Germans, so this time Hermann had to become an Englishman, and he could think of no better name than John Smith. The Italian border guards, who did not speak English, assumed that the Professor's accent was the way all Britons talked, and waved him through customs.

Arriving in La Spezia, a coastal city near Genoa, Hermann put up at a hotel and sent for Tilly. Using the name of Mrs. Smith, entering another country to join her husband, she was not challenged, and again they were together. Each morning he drove to work and returned at dusk to their suite, daring neither to accept social invitations nor mingle with neighbors. It was important that no one connect the silent, gray-haired "Englishman" with Italian military secrets.

## CHAPTER 18

♖  "The space age is moving with nearly escape velocity."  **WILLY LEY**

# The Moon Car
# [1951-1953]

**T**O AID IN HIS DEVELOPMENT of a large powder rocket for anti-aircraft, Hermann hired three Italians and a German chemist from WASAG, who passed as an Englishman named Jones. The Italian Admiralty provided everything needed for the experiments. Hermann's laboratory was in a concrete bunker and for testings he had the use of a rifle range. Actual firings were over marshy ground safe from the presence of alien spies. To thwart spying binoculars, U-boat nets were put up as camouflage. A nearby arsenal factory sent him any chemical he ordered.

By the early part of 1953 his contract ended. What he had accomplished was known only to the Italian Government. He and Tilly had lived frugally, so they had money to take back to Feucht. He was eager to get settled again in his own home and start writing, but they found their house still crowded with bickering refugees. His only work space was the tiny bedside table; his only tools a pencil and paper. He felt lonely. His family was scattered. No word had come from Julius, who was missing on the Russian front, and who has never been heard from. Hermann's elder daughter was a practicing attorney, married, with interest in her own home. Adolf was an independent chemist. Hermann's friends had moved away. His youngest daughter, his father, and his mother were dead. Back where he had started as a young physicist, now at nearly sixty years of age, he had to build a new career.

Since Hermann was not the quitting type he sat down, ignoring the noise about him, and began to write. He tried to recall the scientific ideas he had put into the long manuscript hidden when he had fled WASAG. It had been lost; reports said the advancing Russians used what papers they could find to light their breakfast fires. Because they could not read German many valuable documents went up in flames.

As he reviewed his rocket discoveries, ideas began to take shape and words flowed easily. He called his book *Menschen im Weltraum* (later published in the United States as *Man into Space*). Since he wanted to appeal to ordinary readers, as well as those more scientifically minded, he wrote in a non-technical style, pouring out the richness of his forty years of study. He wanted to make people curious about the mysteries of the planets, to inspire enthusiasm for rocket ships and to show that space travel was not merely possible but a coming reality. That was a big order, he admitted, and he would begin with the place he knew best, the moon.

Despite what the movie *Frau im Mond* had portrayed, man could not explore the moon either on foot or in a conventional vehicle. The terrain was too uncertain. In the sixteenth century certain areas had looked to the Italian astronomer Galileo Galilei like bodies of water, and were given such names as Mare Serenitatis (Sea of Serenity) and Sinus Iridum (Bay of Rainbows). Some of these appeared to be nearly two hundred miles across.

In addition to these mystifying flat regions, the moon had mountains with peaks over three miles high, cut by rills, or cracks, of unknown depth. Then, too, there were surface features unlike anything on the earth. A gorge known as the Great Valley was possibly dug by a grazing meteorite. A strange line called the Straight Wall or Railway was presumably a rocky fault about seventy miles in length. Fanning out from many craters, like spokes from a hub, were mysterious lines called rays, which might be streaks of rock flour shot out by the impact of a meteor or else fused lines of metal.

Like all frontiers, wrote Hermann, this one presents problems never before encountered. First of all, man must design new vehicles to carry him from his homeland. The Pilgrims had the *Mayflower*, equipped for their specific needs during an ocean voyage; the Forty-niners went West in special wagons covered and furnished for particular emergencies on hill or plain. But in crossing the border of the earth's atmosphere, modern pioneers must have radically different transportation, some form of a rocket ship. Nor could they wear ordinary fashions of the day, as did former explorers, buckskins, khakis, or armor.

For airless travel a man would need a special suit. This ought not to fit his body like a skin-diving outfit nor should it be the "silvered rubber" of science fiction. The material must be selected for its resistance to the danger of both radiation and meteoroids. The suit must be adjustable so that the trunk, legs, and arms could be shortened or lengthened. The helmet ought to be equipped with front and side windows and a rear-view mirror. Because these suits would

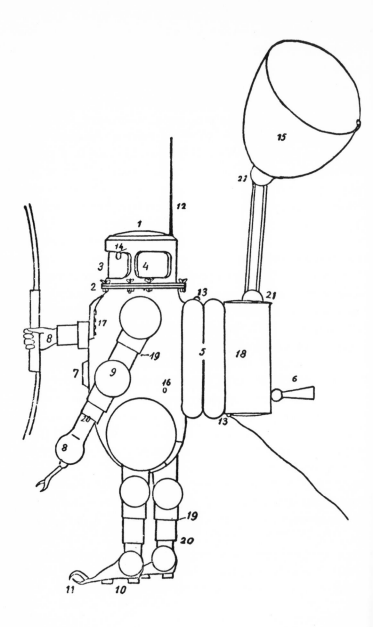

have to be carried from the earth in spaceships, they must be as light in weight as possible.

Only in movies could a man don his space suit and step out of his rocket to repair damage done by a meteoroid. In the real weightlessness of space he could not propel himself by moving his legs. To go forward he would have to apply Newton's law of equal action and reaction. Therefore, he would need a small pistol which would be fired behind him, propelling him forward.

Of course, the cabin of his rocket ship would contain air carried up from the earth. There would also need to be an alarm to warn of a leak. Air is too valuable to permit its escape into space.

While traveling to the moon, pioneers were sure to encounter many dangers. Their ship or space suits might be punctured by meteoroids. Although large meteoroids are rare, dust would be common and could make holes difficult to see with the eye, through which the air could escape.

Arriving on the moon, men would, most astronomers agree, find it covered with an icing of dust. Concerning its depth, estimates vary from a few inches to a mile. This dust could be as treacherous as quicksand or a snowdrift, swallowing up a car and passengers. At other locations, the basic

**Figure 2.** Oberth's proposed space suit. (1) Lid for entry; (2) flange; (3) front window; (4) side window; (5) containers for compressed air and oxygen, and fuel for reaction pistol; (6) reaction pistol; (7) switch panel; (8) glove and claw; (9) joint for elbow; (10) magnets on feet for holding onto spaceship; (11) claw for gripping rungs on spaceship; (12) short-wave aerial; (13) hooks for hanging up the suit; (14) rear-view mirror; (15) heat dissipater; (16) telephone jack; (17) breastplate hinges; (18) flexible air reservoir; (19) adjustment for changing length of leg; (20) rotating joint for ankle; (21) support for heat dissipater. The height of the Moon Car is 18,500 millimeters, approximately 60′ 9″. (Econ-Verlag)

lunar rock shows through. This might prove to be lava, as hard as granite and sharp as glass, or it might be a form of petrified foam easily squashed. Either one would present a perilous roadbed for ordinary wheels, whether bound with solid rubber tires or the hardest metal.

There were yet worse problems for a moon vehicle. Because there is no atmosphere an earth car could not function: engines demand oxygen. Moreover, no one knows the exact effect of moon temperature on a car radiator. In daylight the thermometer would soar over the boiling mark; at night sink to eight times colder than freezing. Under such extremes, engine parts might freeze, snap, or melt. Then, too, the temperature change might harm fuel, oil, and rubber.

To solve such problems, Hermann gathered his information. Since he had already pointed the way into space with his rockets, he decided to go further and design man's transportation after landing.

His moon car would be carried through space on a rocket ship. Instead of wheels, it would have large caterpillar tracks with which to crawl over either rough ground or dust. Above the base would rise a single mast or leg, supporting the cabin, which would ride like an enlarged crow's nest. The entire structure would be kept upright by a powerful gyroscope.

The car could either cruise or jump. It had an automatic device to evaluate a jump and give warning when it was impossible. Although this sounded fantastic, it was relatively simple. The driver sighted through an instrument that recorded the distance. This information was fed into a computing machine that calculated the jump and then passed the calculations on to a robot, which acted. Power for these separate operations would come from the sun's energy, turned into electrical current.

At the end of his section on lunar travel Hermann was able to write:

> I have studied more than 100 details; I have calculated, compared, designed, and replanned until I considered the final design practical enough. Now I can say: "My moon car is ready to be built." Of that I am certain.*

Pioneers would not be too uncomfortable on the moon. They could remain in their spaceship, moon car, and space suits until they had built suitable houses. Living would not be too difficult, since everything would be easy to keep clean. Without air, the moon dust could not blow, and even dust thrown up by the caterpillar tracks would probably fall back like water broken by the bow of a boat. Temperature could be controlled to a certain extent, since it was known that the sun did not heat the "air" but only the objects on which it fell. Giant sunshades would provide protection against the blistering rays. Moreover, by the use of sunshades and space mirrors, the earthly rhythm of day and night could be reproduced.

Moon cabins would be built of prefabricated airtight parts brought from the earth and assembled in a sheltered location or built into partial caves. These houses would be suitable until more permanent settlements could be constructed. The necessary air could be acquired in two possible ways: it could be brought up on cargo ships or released from the moon's rocks. At least one scientist has suggested that under the lunar surface may exist a layer of permanent ice. This could be one of the pleasant surprises awaiting man's arrival. Regardless of what he finds, said Hermann, man can make the moon habitable.

* From *Man into Space*, by Hermann Oberth. New York: Harper and Brothers, 1957, p. 149.

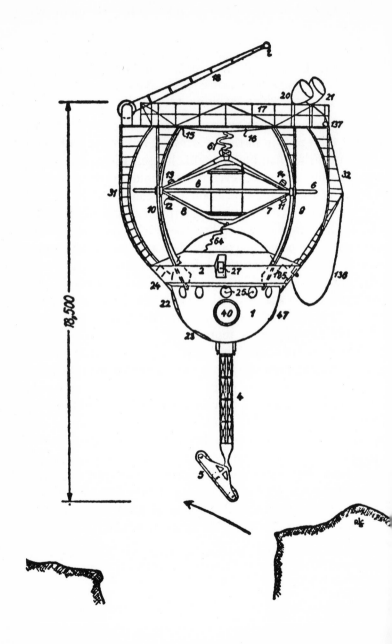

**Figure 3.** The moon car. (1) Cabin; (2) store; (4) leg; (5) driving mechanism; (6) gyroscope; (7) gyroscope frame; (8) mobile gyroscope frame; (9) guides for (7); (10) guides for (8); (11,12) motor for setting (7); (13,14) motor for setting (8); (15) supporting ring; (16) platform; (17) railing; (18) crane; (20) cabin air dissipater; (21) engine heat dissipater; (22) driver's window; (23) floor window; (24) periscope; (25) windows for the crew; (27) mirror before an upper window; (31,32) girders; (40) air locks; (47) outer door refuse ejector; (61) gas pipe to dissipater; (64) electric cable; (135) emergency brake, anchor; (136) emergency brake, cable; (137) emergency brake, roller. (Econ-Verlag)

**CHAPTER 19** ♜ "From my knowledge of the theoretical and experimental sides of the subject, I believe that a rocket from the earth will some day successfully reach one of the planets."

ROBERT H. GODDARD

# Miracles of Space [1954]

T HE YEAR 1954 was a time of unusual events. In Europe Hermann published his book *Menschen im Weltraum;* in America eyes watched the sky, hoping to see one of the reported flying saucers. While some men of integrity claimed to have seen the phenomena in various shapes, the United States Air Force considered them only as Unidentified Flying Objects, or UFO. Excited civilians feared they were Russian spies. Soviet papers insisted "the big saucer bluff" was a Yankee trick to pry research funds from Congress. To get expert opinions, American periodicals consulted numerous scientists, Hermann Oberth among them.

"It is my thesis that flying saucers are real and that they are spaceships from another solar system." *

* From the *American Weekly,* October 24, 1954, p. 4.

Although many young scientists scoffed at the idea, older men recalled that in 1923 they had laughed at Oberth's "nonsense" about rockets. Time had proven the "Grand Old Man of Space" right; perhaps he was at least partially right in this new theory.

Practical citizens were amazed by the notion of another solar system producing intelligent creatures able to navigate space. Yet visionaries claimed that air to mankind might be analogous to water to a fish, and a fish could be taken from the sea and live comfortably in a bowl. Therefore, was it not possible that a human could go into the airless heavens by taking his bowl of air with him? Moreover, it was conceivable that creatures had evolved which lived in an atmosphere composed of gases other than oxygen and nitrogen. Science fiction took on a façade of truth. Everyone demanded facts about the envelope encasing the earth.

Up to ten miles above the ground it is possible for men to breathe; above twelve miles the pressure is so low that liquids, including the blood, boil at about ninety-eight degrees. At fifteen miles the atmosphere contains ozone, poisonous in large doses. So there was no doubt that if man expected to explore distant planets, he would need to carry his air with him.

Assuming that he could successfully escape the earth's gravity, he would immediately meet another problem. Since the planets are too far away to be reached without a rest stop for fuel and supplies, the space travelers would need a "halfway house," as on the old stagecoach lines. There is no better place to build such a depot than on one of the thousands of asteroids, or minor planets. These are rocky bodies that possibly might contain artifacts of extinct beings. They vary in size from chunks less than a mile in diameter to Ceres, which has a mean diameter of about five hundred miles. With few exceptions, these asteroids travel in orbits around the sun between Mars and Jupiter. Their origin remains a mystery. Many astronomers believe they are unformed fragments of a planet strangely missing from the earth's solar system. Some think a planet broke apart in its orbit millions of years ago. Hermann studied this enigma by looking not only into the past, but also into the future. He wrote:

> People with imaginative minds even speculate as to whether this vanished planet was blown into the air (or rather, into space) by its own inhabitants, and this idea is put forward as a timely warning. Within the foreseeable future the earth's inhabitants will unquestionably have the means and the power of blowing their own planet to pieces.*

These asteroids provide ready-made airports on which spaceships can land. One could even be captured and towed to another place to serve as a quarry for raw material in building a station. It would be easier to use the stone and metal found on an asteroid than to haul them up from the earth.

Once a station is established, it could be used as a depot for flights into the interplanetary regions. There would be other uses for such a space port. Experiments which are either too dangerous or impossible on the earth could be performed in space; for example, tests involving extremely high temperatures or the lack of gravity. No doubt botanists would be interested in learning the influence of gravity on plants, which without gravity might grow to giant size. The science of astronomy would be aided by a telescope on a space station, where there would be no distortion in observation due to atmosphere. Moreover, with little gravity, tele-

* From *Man into Space*, by Hermann Oberth. New York: Harper and Brothers, 1957, p. 156.

scopes of vast lengths and diameters could be built. On the earth large telescopes are heavy and must be reinforced to prevent bending. This would be unnecessary in space. In addition, a space station could act as a broadcasting or television link between points far removed on the earth by reflecting the beams from one to the other.

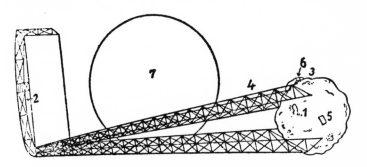

**Figure 4.** The space telescope. (1) Asteroid; (2) objective mirror; (3) observatory; (4) frame; (5) swivel-mounted rocket nozzle; (6) photoelectric cell arrangement for following the object focused; (7) movable screen for preventing sunlight from reaching the objective. (Econ-Verlag)

The power to operate a space station is already available in energy from the sun, and some day it will be possible to draw power from the sun in huge amounts.

These are only some part of the miracles scheduled for the future. As Hermann wrote:

It is possible that men will one day reach distant, unknown planets of other suns. They will travel the colossal distance in roller stations, in communities they themselves had established, and would reach their goal thousands of years later. . . . On reaching their destination, the descendants of those who had set out would explore the planets and open them for their successors. Memories of their ancestral earth, which they would know only as a planet far below in the depth of space, would be hazy and unreal; the story of earthly man on microfilm and recording tapes would be thought of by these spacemen as we think of fanciful fairy tales from the legendary world of the dead.*

* From *Man into Space*, by Hermann Oberth. New York: Harper and Brothers, 1957, p. 166.

**CHAPTER 20** ♜ "The wise man looks into space, and does not regard the small as too little, nor the great as too big; for he knows there is no limit to dimensions."

LAO-TSE

# *Honors to the Father of Space Travel* [1955-1961]

I N THE SPRING of 1955 the townspeople of Feucht noticed more American officers than usual about their streets. Then they discovered that large cars were driving up to the *Schloss*, or "little castle," of the Oberths. After a few days the visitors vanished as abruptly as they had appeared. Following them, Hermann and Tilly departed. Only then did the village learn that the Professor had been invited by Dr. von Braun to work on rockets in the United States.

The couple arrived in New York on a hot day in July, 1955. With a minimum of the usual immigration red tape they went to Huntsville, Alabama (Plate 13), to join the team of scientists working under the direction of Dr. von Braun. To Hermann's delight he found himself once more among his companions from Peenemünde. The one difference was that now he was applying his rocket knowledge for the U.S. Army Ordnance Corps.

Life in his cottage on Hermitage Street in Huntsville was pleasant for Hermann. His fellow Germans were loyal to their newly adopted flag, although the road to their citizenship in the United States had not been easy. No group had been looked upon with more suspicion than these "Operation Paper Clip" men who began to arrive in 1945. They had to prove themselves worthy of becoming American citizens. To do so, they not only learned English but took part in community affairs, in church work, music, and other cultural activities.

Later, when the Germans brought their families to this country, the children heard taunts at school about being Nazis. Never had German fighting blood been called upon for more patience.

Because these men were technically under military custody they had no official status. Nor could their waiting time for citizenship begin until they had officially emigrated to the United States. To fulfill that requirement, many were taken to Mexico and brought back through border customs, so that about the time Hermann arrived, his friends were having parties to celebrate becoming naturalized citizens.

He found all America excited over its satellite program. It was easy for him to catch the enthusiasm, for he discovered that the flight into orbit was based on rocket principles he had proclaimed more than thirty years earlier (Plate 14).

"In fact," he was to write later, "I am rather surprised that so many of my former suggestions have been adopted in modern rocket development. Among others, only these should be mentioned: Regenerative cooling, reinforcing tanks by internal pressure, liquid fuels such as alcohol containing water and liquid oxygen . . . and, finally, the use of liquid hydrogen as fuel in upper stages." *

The publication of his book *Man into Space* in 1957 put his name into almost every library. He also had another reason to feel happy. His son, a chemist, had come to make his home in the United States. Then, too, world scientists were proving that the first of his propositions written in 1923 was true: ". . . *it is possible to build machines which can climb higher than the earth's atmosphere.*" The Russians had sent aloft their Sputnik and proved his second assertion true: ". . . *these machines can reach such speed that if left in space they will not fall back to the earth but will be able to resist the pull of gravity.*" Already there was talk of putting a man into space, which would support his third statement: "*These machines can be built so that men can go up in them (probably without danger to their bodies).*"

His life was still not free from trouble, however. As a former civil employee he received a pension from Germany, but German law forbade sending that money to a man living in a foreign country. He did not want to forfeit that income, since he had passed the age where he could build up a retirement pension in a new land. By American rules he had to retire at the age of sixty-five which left him less than four years to work for the government; his pension from this would scarcely buy the paper and pens he needed for his writing. The only chance to remain in the United States after his army work had finished was by finding private employment. Tilly also favored this so that they could be near their son.

* From "Hermann Oberth—From My Life" by Hermann Oberth *Astronautics* (June 1959), p. 101.

Once more he placed his application with firms which might need a technical advisor or mathematician. Repeatedly there came back excuses why he could not be hired. Dr. von Braun and Major General J. B. Medaris, the Commanding General of the Army Ballistic Missile Agency, tried to get him a research grant from one of the great foundations, but failed. No one wanted to employ his trained mind. It seemed that men were swayed by his wrinkles and gray hair. All his life he had experienced rejections, but he had learned to bear them and still carry on. He could remember his own words, uttered at the close of World War II when all doors were closed to him.

"All my attempts to find a job as teacher in University, high school or even public school were futile. I guess I can do nothing better than grow cabbages and turnips in my vegetable garden." *

The Father of Space Travel was forced to return to his home in Feucht. Perhaps the actual building of his rockets were meant for younger hands, which he would inspire with his plans. With equations he could continue to build a bridge for the feet of Tomorrow, a bridge from the earth to distant space. Whether the world remembered him did not matter. He had made his contribution to progress. Continuing the work he had begun, other men might someday reach the planets around distant suns.

And for what purpose? Hermann gave his answer in *Man into Space*.

"This is the goal: To make available for life every place where life is possible. To make inhabitable all worlds as yet uninhabitable, and all life purposeful." †

In 1961 Hermann was honored from both sides of the

* From "Beyond the News," *U.N. World* (November, 1952), p. 9.
† From *Man into Space*, by Hermann Oberth, New York: Harper and Brothers, 1957, p. 167.

Atlantic (Plate 16). The West German Government gave him its highest award to a scientist, the Great Cross of Merit (Plate 15). And an American school, the Iowa Wesleyan College, presented him with a degree, making him at last Dr. Hermann Oberth.

# Glossary

**A-1**   The first rocket built by the Dornberger-von Braun team. It was tested but never launched.

**A-4**   See V-2.

**American Rocket Society**   A pioneer American society for research into rocketry, founded in 1930 as the American Interplanetary Society.

**Asteroid**   A small body circling the sun between the orbits of Mars and Jupiter. There are thousands of asteroids, which may be fragments of a distintegrated or unformed planet.

**Astronautics**   The science of flight and navigation in space.

**Atmosphere**   The layer of gases surrounding the earth to a height of approximately 120 miles.

**Ballistics**   The science dealing with the motion of projectiles and missiles.

**Booster Rocket**   A rocket used to supply extra thrust in take-off, after which it falls away from the main rocket.

**British Interplanetary Society**   The English counterpart of The German Rocket Society.

**Combustion Chamber**   That part of a rocket motor in which fuels are mixed and burned, a tank made of stainless steel.

**Cosmic Rays**   Atomic nuclei that bombard the earth with high penetrating power. Ninety-five percent are believed to originate in the sun.

**Escape Velocity**   The minimum speed needed for any object to escape from the earth's gravitational force: seven miles per second.

**Exhaust Velocity**   The speed at which burned gases leave the nozzle of a combustion chamber.

**Film Cooling**   A system for cooling by injecting fuel into the nozzle to form a heat-protective film. Also called veil cooling.

151

**Fin**  A winglike device which stabilizes the rocket in flight.

**Firing Chamber**  A combustion chamber.

**Free Fall**  The powerless coasting of a spaceship, *or* the falling of an object under the force of gravity alone.

**Fuel**  A substance which is burned with air or oxygen to produce heat and gas.

**German Rocket Society**  A pioneer society for rocket research, founded in 1927.

**Gravity**  The force with which a celestial body attracts another object. The force is in direct proportion to the masses of the bodies and in indirect proportion to the square of the distance between them.

**Guided Missile**  A missile capable of being guided by remote control from the ground.

**Gyroscope**  A device employing a spinning wheel or disk, used to control the balance of a rocket or spaceship. A gyroscope resists any change in direction at right angles to the plane of spin.

**Ionosphere**  A layer of ionized or electrically charged gases extending from 50 to 400 miles above the earth.

**Jupiter**  The largest planet in the earth's solar system, with a diameter eleven times that of the earth. It is the fifth planet from the sun.

**Launching Pad**  The complex of permanent machinery from which a rocket is fired into space.

**Light-Year**  The distance traveled by light in one solar year. About six trillion miles.

**Liquid Oxygen**  Oxygen in liquid form, prepared by cooling the gas. Used for rocket fuel.

**Liquid Propellant**  A combination of fuel and liquid oxygen.

**Mars**  The fourth planet from the sun, with a diameter half that of the earth.

**Meteor**  The entering of the earth's atmosphere by a particle of matter from space traveling at high speed. The compression of the air in its path heats it and causes it to glow.

**Meteorite**  A meteoric body which has fallen upon the earth.

**Meteoroid**  A subplanetary particle of matter in outer space.

**Nozzle**  The vent or spout through which the gases escape from a combustion chamber. The nozzle is so shaped as to increase the speed of the gases.

**Orbit**  The fixed path of a smaller celestial body around a larger one.

**Outer Space**  That portion of the universe beyond the immediate influence of the earth and its atmosphere.

**Oxidizer**  A substance that supplies oxygen to a fuel for combustion.

**Oxygen**  An element in the air necessary for breathing and combustion. Approximately one-fifth of the air is oxygen.

**Payload**  The cargo of a rocket.

**Peenemünde**  A famous World War II German rocket center on the Baltic Sea, where the V-2 was developed.

**Propellant**  The fuel plus the oxidizer, in liquid or solid form, used to produce gas in a rocket motor.

**Radar**  An electronic device that detects objects by transmitting a radio beam and measuring the energy reflected by the object. It can be used in any weather, day or night.

**Regenerative Cooling**  A method in which the propellant is used for cooling before being burned.

**Rocket**  A jet-propelled vehicle designed to travel above the earth's surface. It carries its own oxidizer and so does not depend on air for its oxygen.

**Rocket Motor**  The basic elements of the rocket motor are the combustion chamber and exhaust nozzle. The propellant is burned in the chamber, liberating gases that are discharged through the nozzle, driving the motor forward.

**Servomotors**  The small motors in a rocket that operate the various mechanisms.

**Solid Propellant**  A fuel in the form of powder or cake.

**Space Flight**  Flight beyond the atmosphere.

**Spaceship**  A manned vehicle designed to travel in outer space.

**Space Station**  A depot in space for research, refueling, observation, and so on.

**Static Test**  The testing of a rocket that is held stationary on the ground in a stand.

**Step Rockets**  Several rockets connected in such a way that when one burns out it ignites the next. The burned-out rocket then falls away. Also called multistage rockets.

**Supersonic Speed**  A speed faster than the speed of sound: approximately 740 miles per hour.

**Test Stand**  A metal or cement structure that holds a rocket on the ground while it is being tested or examined.

**Thrust**  The force that propels a rocket or missile.

**Upper Atmosphere**  The ionosphere.

**V-1**  A small, pilotless airplane containing a warhead, made by Germany during World War II. It was not a true rocket, since it depended on air for its oxygen.

**V-2**  A German military rocket, originally called the A-4, developed during World War II. The V-2 was forty-six feet long and fueled with a mixture of grain alcohol and water; its maximum speed was about 3600 miles per hour. Over three thousand fell on London during the War.

**Viking**   An American rocket sponsored by the United States Navy and patterned on the V-2.

**Warhead**   The section of a rocket containing explosives, usually the nose.

**Weightlessness**   A condition of zero gravity in which objects float freely in space. It occurs when gravity is counteracted, as in free fall, or where gravity is infinitesimal, as in interplanetary space.

# Synoptic Calendar

| | | |
|---|---|---|
| Hermann Oberth born June 25 at Hermannstadt, Transylvania (now Rumania). | **1894** | *Republic of Hawaii proclaimed.* |
| Family moved to Schaessburg. | **1896** | *William McKinley elected President of the United States.* |
| | **1898** | *Spanish-American War.* |
| Hermann made drawings of inventions in his secret notebook. | **1899** | |
| Went to school in Schaessburg. | **1902** | |
| | **1904** | *Russo-Japanese War began.* |
| Began to read Jules Verne, and studied Verne's spaceship. | **1906** | *Lee De Forest invented the vacuum tube.* |
| Graduated from Schaessburg school with a prize in mathematics. | **1912** | *Woodrow Wilson elected American President. Titanic sunk in Atlantic Ocean.* |
| Entered the University of Munich. | **1913** | *End of the Balkan Wars.* |
| Joined the Austro-Hungarian Army. | **1914** | *World War I began. United States neutral.* |

1917 — *Russian Revolution. United States entered War.*

Offered the German War Department a plan for a long-range rocket missile; his offer rejected. Married Mathilde Hummel in July.

1918 — *End of World War I. Armistice. Communist Government established in Russia.*

Discharged from the army. Entered the University of Munich. Son Julius born.

1919 — *Treaty of Versailles signed.*

Proposed a space station to refuel spaceships.

1920 — *Warren G. Harding elected President of the United States.*

Studied at the University of Göttingen.

1921 — *Burial of America's Unknown Soldier.*

Studied at Heidelberg University. Daughter Erna born.

1922 — *Dedication of Lincoln Memorial in Washington, D.C.*

*Die Raket zu den Planetenräumen* published. Hermann taught at Schaessburg.

1923 — *President Harding died. Calvin Coolidge became President of the United States.*

Taught at Mediasch. Daughter Ilse born.

1924 — *Calvin Coolidge elected President. Hitler wrote Mein Kampf.*

Joined The German Rocket Society.

1927 — *Charles Lindbergh flew the Atlantic.*

Went to Berlin as technical advisor for film, *Frau im Mond*. Son Adolf born.

1928 — *Herbert Hoover elected President of the United States. The Graf Zeppelin flew to the United States from Germany.*

Awarded the REP-Hirsch prize. His book *Wege zur Raumschiffahrt* published.

1929 — *Great Depression began with collapse of American stock market.*

| | | |
|---|---|---|
| Demonstrated a liquid-fuel rocket. | **1930** | *American Interplanetary Society formed.* |
| Predicted mail service from Europe to America by rocket. | **1931** | *Depression worsened. Shadows of another war.* |
| Refused to work for Russia. | **1932** | *Franklin D. Roosevelt elected President of the United States. Nazi Party won majority in German elections.* |
| Refused offer to work for Japan. | **1934** | |
| Told German officers about his anti-aircraft missile. | **1935** | *Hitler abrogated the Versailles Treaty.* |
| | **1936** | *Rome-Berlin Axis formed.* |
| | **1937** | *Work begun at Peenemünde.* |
| Did research at Technical University in Vienna. | **1938** | *Munich agreement.* |
| | **1939** | *World War II begun. Soviet-German non-aggression pact.* |
| Research work at Technical University in Dresden. | **1940** | *Roosevelt re-elected President for third term. German troops entered Paris.* |
| Consulting engineer at Peenemünde. His mother died. | **1941** | *Hitler attacked Russia. Japan attacked Pearl Harbor. United States declared war.* |
| Hermann received the Cross of Merit with swords. Worked for WASAG. Son Julius missing in Russia. | **1943** | *England's bombers razed Peenemünde. Italy surrendered. Casablanca Conference.* |
| Daughter Ilse died in war accident. Son Adolf called to war. | **1944** | *Roosevelt elected for fourth term. Mass V-2 attack on London.* |

| | |
|---|---|
| Captured by Allies. Released. Went home to Feucht. | **1945** *End of World War II. First atom bomb. Death of President Roosevelt.* |
| Teacher, writer, and technical advisor. Difficult times. | **1946** *Captured German scientists brought to the United States. V-2's fired at White Sands.* |
| Worked in Switzerland as technical advisor, teacher, and writer. | **1948** *Harry Truman elected President of the United States. Russia working on captured V-2 rockets.* |
| Made honorary member of the British Interplanetary Society and honorary president of the German Society for Space Research. | **1949** *North Atlantic Pact signed by twelve nations. United Nations headquarters dedicated.* |
| Worked for the Italian Government. German Society for Space Research founded the Oberth Medal for outstanding work on astronautics. | **1950** *War in Korea. Russia began to produce rockets and guided missiles.* |
| | **1952** *Dwight D. Eisenhower elected President of the United States. United States exploded first hydrogen bomb.* |
| Completed work in Italy and returned home to Feucht. | **1953** *Korean Armistice signed.* |
| *Menschen im Weltraum* published. Acknowledged as civil servant entitled to German pension. Received the Diesel Medal. Detroit Rocket Society made him technical director. | **1954** *First atomic-powered submarine. Anti-polio vaccine put into use.* |

Joined von Braun's team at Redstone Arsenal. Received the Space Flight Award of the American Astronautical Society.

**1955** *Racial segregation in public schools banned by Supreme Court of the United States.*

Received the Pendray Award of the American Rocket Society. His son, Adolf, came to the United States.

**1956** *Eisenhower re-elected President.*

*Man into Space* published in America.

**1957** *International Geophysical Year. Russia launched Sputnik.*

Retired to Germany.

**1958** *First United States satellite, Explorer One, launched. Alaska admitted as a state.*

*The Moon Car* published in America.

**1959** *Hawaii admitted into the United States.*

Received the Great Cross of Merit, highest given by the German Government to a scientist. Received a Doctorate from Iowa Wesleyan College.

**1961** *Russia launched first man into space.*

Awarded the Galabert Prize for achievement in the field of astronautics in France.

**1962** *United States launched a man into space.*

# Bibliography

## BOOKS

Baedeker, K., *Austria, including Hungary, Dalmatia, Bosnia*. New York: Charles Scribner's Sons, 1911.

Balchen, Bernt and Bergaust, Erik, *The Next Fifty Years of Flight*. New York: Harper and Brothers, 1954.

Baumbach, Werner, *Life and Death of the Luftwaffe*. New York: Coward-McCann, Inc., 1960.

Bell, Joseph N., *Seven into Space*. Chicago: Popular Mechanics Co., 1960.

Bergaust, Erik, *Reaching for the Stars*. New York: Doubleday & Company, Inc., 1960.

Bergaust, Erik, *Rockets to the Moon*. New York: G. P. Putnam's Sons, 1961.

Caiden, Martin, *Vanguard*. New York: E. P. Dutton & Co., Inc., 1957.

Castor, H., *America's First World War*. Eau Claire, Wisconsin: E. M. Hale, 1957.

Clarke, Arthur C., *The Exploration of Space*. New York: Harper and Brothers, 1959.

Cornish, Louis C., *Transylvania*. Philadelphia: Dorrance, 1947.

Crosse, A. T., *Round About the Carpathians*. Edinburgh: William Blackwood, 1878.

Deuel, Wallace R., *People under Hitler*. New York: Harcourt, Brace & Company, Inc., 1942.

Dornberger, Walter, V-2. New York: Viking Press, Inc., 1954.

Foisel, John, *Saxons through Seventeen Centuries*. Cleveland: Central Alliance of Transylvanian Saxons of U.S., 1936.

Fromm, Bella, *Blood and Banquets*. New York: Harper and Brothers, 1942.

161

Gartman, Heinz, *Men Behind the Space Rockets*. London: Weidenfeld & Nicolson, 1955.

Gatland, Kenneth W., *Project Satellite*. London: Allan Wingate, 1958.

Gatland, Kenneth W. and Kunesch, Anthony, *Space Travel*. New York: Philosophical Library, 1953.

Goddard, Robert H., *Rocket Development*. New York: Prentice-Hall, Inc., 1948.

Goodwin, Hal, *Real Book about Space Travel*. New York: Doubleday & Company, Inc., 1956.

Haley, Andrew G., *Rocketry and Space Exploration*. New York: D. Van Nostrand Company, Inc., 1958.

Humphries, John, *Rockets and Guided Missiles*. New York: The Macmillan Company, 1956.

Lang, Daniel, *From Hiroshima to the Moon*. New York: Simon & Schuster, Inc., 1959.

Leonard, Jonathan N., *Flight into Space*. New York: Random House, Inc., 1953.

Levitt, Israel M., *Target for Tomorrow*. New York: Fleet Publishing Corp., 1959.

Ley, Willy, *Rockets and Space Travel*. New York: Viking Press, Inc., 1944.

Ley, Willy, *Rockets, Missiles and Space Travel*. New York: Viking Press, Inc., 1961.

Mallan, Lloyd, *Men, Rockets and Space Rats*. New York: Julian Messner, Inc., 1955.

Maco Magazine Corp., *The Complete Book of Outer Space*. New York: Jerry Mason, 1953.

Medaris, Gen. John B., *Countdown for Decision*. New York: G. P. Putnam's Sons, 1960.

Moore, Patrick, *Earth Satellites*. New York: W. W. Norton & Company, Inc., 1956.

Oberth, Hermann, *Man into Space*. New York: Harper and Brothers, 1957.

Oberth, Hermann, *The Moon Car*. New York: Harper and Brothers, 1959.

Oberth, Hermann, *Wege zur Raumschiffahrt* ("Road to Space Travel"). München: R. Oldenbourg, 1929.

Pinson, Koppel S., *Modern Germany*. New York: The Macmillan Company, 1954.

Parry, Albert, *Russia's Rockets and Missiles*. New York: Doubleday & Company, Inc., 1960.

Poole, Lynn, *Your Trip into Space*. New York: McGraw-Hill Book Company, Inc., 1953.

Rosen, Milton W., *The Viking Rocket Story*. New York: Harper and Brothers, 1955.

Ryan, Cornelius, *Across the Space Frontier*. New York: Viking Press, Inc., 1952.

Schussler, Eileen and Raymond, *Starbound*. New York: G. P. Putnam's Sons, 1960.

Schutz and Levine, *German Home Front*. London: Victor Gollancz, Ltd., 1943.

Snyder, Louis L., *The First Book of World War I*. New York: Franklin Watts, Inc., 1958.

Snyder, Louis L., *The First Book of the Soviet Union*. New York: Franklin Watts, Inc., 1959.

Staff Report, *Space Handbook: Aeronautics and Its Applications*. U.S. Govt. Printing Office, 1959.

Starkie, Walter Fitzwilliam, *Raggle-Taggle*. New York: E. P. Dutton & Co., Inc., 1933.

Stehling, K. R., *Project Vanguard*. New York: Doubleday & Company, Inc., 1961.

Stine, George H., *Rocket Power and Space Flight*. New York: Henry Holt & Company, Inc., 1957.

Sutton, George P., *Rocket Propulsion Elements*. New York: John Wiley & Sons, Inc., 1949.

Thomas, Shirley, *Men of Space*. Philadelphia: Chilton Company, 1960, 1961.

Tregaskis, Richard W., *X-15 Diary*. New York: E. P. Dutton & Co., Inc., 1961.

Verne, Jules, *From the Earth to the Moon*. New York: Globe Book Company, Inc., 1958.

Weiser, William J., *Space Guidebook*. New York: Coward-McCann, Inc., 1960.

Williams, Beryl and Epstein, Samuel, *Rocket Pioneers*. New York: Julian Messner, Inc., 1958.

Woodbury, David O., *Around the World in 90 Minutes*. New York: Harcourt, Brace & Company, Inc., 1958.

Yates, Raymond F. and Russell, M. E., *Space Rockets and Missiles*. New York: Harper and Brothers, 1960.

Zwicky, Fritz, *Report on Certain Phases of War Research in Germany*. Headquarters Air Materiel Command, 1947.

## ARTICLES

"Beyond the News," *U.N. World* (November, 1952), p. 9.

Goudsmit, S. A., "Nazis' Atomic Secrets," *Life*, (October 20, 1947), p. 123.

Johnson, Alvin, "Refugee Scientists," *New Republic* (June 28, 1954), p. 22.

Kent, George, "The Man Who Saved London," *Reader's Digest* (September, 1961), p. 230.

Lang, Daniel, "A Reporter at Large," *New Yorker* (April 21, 1951), p. 75.

Ley, Willy, "Father of Astronautics," *Saturday Review* (September 1, 1956), p. 42.

*Life* (December 9, 1946), p. 49.

Mac Cormac, John, "Scientist Predicts War with Rockets," *New York Times* (January 31, 1931), p. 8.

"Moon Car Jumps Chasms" *Science News Letter* (October 24, 1959), p. 270.

Nagan, Seymour, "Top Secret: Nazis at Work," *New Republic* (August 11, 1947), p. 24.

Oberth, Hermann, "Hermann Oberth—An Autobiography," *Astronautics* (June, 1959), p. 38.

Oberth, Hermann, "Flying Saucers Come from a Distant World," *American Weekly* (October 24, 1954), p. 4.

Oberth, Hermann, "Why the Race to the Moon?", *American Weekly* (October 2, 1955) p. 7.

O'Hallaren, Bill, "Department of Further Amplification," *New Yorker* (May 26, 1951), p. 106.

"A Rocket Expert," *U.S. News and World Report* (July 15, 1955), p. 16.

"Rocket Pioneers—The Army's Team," *U.S. News and World Report* (February 7, 1958), p. 35.

"Secrets from Hitler," *Newsweek* (December 9, 1946), p. 22.

"Space Mirror," *Time* (April 5, 1954), p. 77.

"Spoils of War," *Newsweek* (February 10, 1958), p. 32.

Whelihan, Peter J., "German Genius Pays a Debt," *The Nation's Business* (May, 1949), p. 76.

# Index

## ABOUT THE AUTHOR

**Dr. Helen B. Walters** has written a number of distinguished scientific biographies, including *Nikola Tesla: Giant of Electricity*. A world-traveler, she was born in Portage, Wisconsin, and now lives in Los Angeles, California.

HERMANN OBERTH: FATHER OF SPACE TRAVEL is the first full-length biography in the English language of this pioneer of rocket-flight technique, who helped to create the Space Age in which we live. In the preparation of her biography, Helen B. Walters worked closely with Dr. Oberth and his family, which placed various documents at her disposal and gave her valuable assistance.